Grassland studies

PRACTICAL ECOLOGY SERIES

Seashore Studies
Urban Ecology
Grassland Studies
Freshwater Studies
Woodland Studies

Series editor

Morton Jenkins, B.Sc., M.I.Biol.

Head of Science, Howardian High School, Cardiff
Chief examiner W.J.E.C. in CSE Biology
Examiner C.U.E.S.

TITLES OF RELATED INTEREST

Energy Flow in Ecosystems
Estimating the Size of Animal Populations
Statistics Tables

Grassland studies

Juliet Brodie
Dale Fort Field Centre, nr Haverfordwest

London
GEORGE ALLEN & UNWIN
Boston   Sydney

George Allen & Unwin (Publishers) Ltd,
40 Museum Street, London WC1A 1LU, UK

George Allen & Unwin (Publishers) Ltd,
Park Lane, Hemel Hempstead, Herts HP2 4TE, UK

Allen & Unwin Inc.,
Fifty Cross Street, Winchester, Mass. 01890, USA

George Allen & Unwin Australia Pty Ltd,
8 Napier Street, North Sydney, NSW 2060, Australia

First published in 1985

ISSN 0261–0493

British Library Cataloguing in Publication Data

Brodie, Juliet
    Grassland studies.——(Practical ecology series,
ISSN 0261-0493;3)
1. Grassland ecology——Great Britain
I. Title
574.5′2643′0941   QH137
ISBN 0-04-574020-8

Library of Congress Cataloging in Publication Data

Brodie, Juliet.
    Grassland studies.
(Practical ecology series, ISSN 0261-0493;3)
Bibliography: p.
Includes index.
Summary: A guide for studying grassland ecology, with exercises for
direct involvement in analyzing vegetation, animal life, soil, energy flow,
and climatic factors.
1. Grassland ecology——Field work. 2.
Grassland-ecology——Laboratory manuals. 3. Grassland
ecology——Problems, exercises, etc. [1. Grassland ecology. 2. Ecology]
I. Title. II. Series: Practical ecology.
QH541.5.P7B756 1985   574.5′2643   84-14655
ISBN 0-04-574020-8 (pbk.:alk. paper)

Set in 10 on 12pt Times by
D. P. Media Limited, Hitchin, Hertfordshire
and printed in Great Britain by Mackays of Chatham

Foreword

The aim of this series is to provide students and teachers of Advanced level biological science with ideas for a practical approach to ecology. Each book deals with a particular ecosystem and has been written by an experienced teacher who has had a particular interest in organising and teaching field work. The texts include:

(a) an introduction to the ecosystem studied;
(b) keys necessary for the identification of organisms used in the practical work;
(c) background information relevant to field and laboratory studies;
(d) descriptions of methods and techniques used in the practical exercises;
(e) lists of materials needed for the practical work described;
(f) realistic suggestions for the amount of time necessary to complete each exercise;
(g) a series of questions to be answered with knowledge gained from an investigatory approach to the study;
(h) a bibliography for further reference.

Throughout the series emphasis is placed on *understanding* the ecology, rather than on compiling lists, of organisms. The identification of types, with the use of keys is intended to be a means to an end rather than an end in itself.

Morton Jenkins
Series editor

Preface

Grasslands provide some of the most interesting and readily available habitats for the student wishing to study the principles of ecology. The exercises in this book are designed to be carried out in any accessible area of grassland, for example playing fields, lawns and grassland verges, and should enable many students to pursue the subject with ease.

The methods described are intended for use at sixth-form level. They aim to use the minimum of equipment for the maximum return of information, and lend themselves to further short-term investigations as well as long-term project work.

Juliet Brodie

Acknowledgements

The writing of this book has caused me to be indebted to a number of people. I would like to thank Lucy Evans, who has done the bulk of the typing and provided useful advice. Next I would like to thank all my colleagues at Dale Fort Field Centre, in particular Teresa Bennett, Peter Wyles and John Archer-Thompson who have been invaluable in the later stages, as well as encouragement from David Emerson. I am grateful to all the students who have participated in fieldwork related to this text and in helping to collect real data for the tables and graphs. I would like to mention especially the girls from Howells School, Cardiff who have visited the Centre over the past few years. I am grateful to Pat Morris for reviewing the typescript. Finally, my thanks go to Morton Jenkins and Miles Jackson for help and encouragement whenever needed.

Contents

Introduction

Without the influence of man, it is likely that grasslands as we know them would not exist today. Apart from the maritime, submaritime and mountain communities, much of Britain would originally have been covered by trees. The range of grasses and associated species would have been restricted to open areas within the woodland. As man cleared the forests and began to keep livestock, grazing and trampling by his animals would have prevented the regeneration of trees, allowing grasses and other flowering plants to become more widely established.

Skilful management and development throughout the centuries has created and maintained the present range of grasslands. If the activities of man ceased, a natural sequence of vegetation replacement, known as succession, would take place. Most areas would be invaded by woody species which would outcompete the grassland plants until a stable woodland community was established. This would be the climatic climax vegetation, determined mainly by climate. Grasslands therefore represent a biotic climax, held in balance directly or indirectly by man.

Successful management and maintenance not only involve a consideration of the living vegetation, but also the relationship of that vegetation with its surroundings; in other words an understanding of the ecology of grasslands. This implies a knowledge of the non-living or physical environment – the shape of the land, the soil and the climate – and the role it plays in shaping the living environment. Soil is fundamental to plant life and much of the difference between successful and unsuccessful farming has been due to the varying degree of compatibility between grassland requirements and soil properties. It provides nutrients, water and support, as well as being a habitat for such organisms as bacteria, fungi and earthworms, that are instrumental in decomposing dead organic matter, thus recycling essential materials.

Grassland falls into two broad categories: agricultural land (including moors and downs for rough grazing, and cultivated rich permanent pasture), and recreational land (lawns, parks and playing fields). This variety plays a major part in the appearance of the British landscape.

Grasses naturally dominate the grassland sward, although the number of grass species present may be small. Their meristematic or growing regions are at the base of the leaf blades and so will continue to grow while their tips are being eaten. Grasses are also able to tiller, which means that there is an increase in the number of shoots without a marked lengthening of the stem. This enables the grass to spread rapidly forming a resistant mat, as well as producing soft, palatable shoots. They are therefore well adapted to withstand the main pressures of grazing and trampling.

The dependence of man on grasslands for food cannot be over-emphasised. Grass varieties have been selected and developed to fulfil the needs of the farmers, who require grasses of high productivity, balanced nutritional value, high palatability and persistence for the maintenance of livestock. From a recreational point of view, the gardener requires tough, persistent species for lawns, and sometimes ornamental grasses with aesthetic qualities. Playing fields need resilient grasses having a good recovery potential after rough treatment.

There are over one hundred species of grass thought to be native to Britain, but only about twelve are important from an agricultural point of view. One species in particular, perennial rye grass (*Lolium perenne*), is extremely widespread, and flourishes in well-managed pastures, often out-competing many other species. Grasses are only a part of the flora of grasslands, other species of flowering plants often being present in large numbers. Some species have an agricultural value, for example white/Dutch clover (*Trifolium repens*), which is often planted together with rye grass for grazing purposes. Sometimes poor management may lead to the introduction of unwanted plants or weeds, such as buttercups and thistles. Other species, for example snakeshead fritillary (*Fritillaria meleagris*), are confined to meadows and pastures, and indeed are characteristic of them.

Thus grasslands are important from an agricultural, as well as an ecological, standpoint, providing a habitat for both plants and their dependent animals. Chalk grassland, for example, supports a very rich flora including many rare species.

Rapid and marked changes in latter years, away from traditional to modern farming methods, have led to a decline in the haymeadows and pastures that supported a wealth of wildlife, and an increase in areas that are seeded with a single or a few species. This, coupled with increased use of fertilisers, herbicides and pesticides, has led to the destruction or reduction of many grassland species.

Our hope for study lies in the remaining grassland verges, hedgerows, gardens, parks and playing fields, and this book aims to explore these habitats through a series of practical exercises. The book is divided into sections covering ecological analysis of the vegetation and animals, decomposition, energy flow, topography, climate and soils.

The sections are intended to be inter-related, and for comparative purposes the exercises are best carried out on a variety of grasslands. In this way students should gain a better understanding of the ecological significance of different aspects of the grasslands.

Introduction to a grassland site

Background

The topography or shape of any lawn, playing field or rough pasture is unique. Features of the topography include the bedrock, and the site's aspect, gradient and altitude. The bedrock provides the material for the overlying soil, and hence influences the physical and chemical nature of the soil. Bedding planes and joints within the bedrock may improve drainage, and provide access for plant roots and shelter for animal life. The gradient or steepness of a site (which can be measured by the angle of the slope), will affect the drainage and stability of the substrate, and hence the colonising ability of plants.

The aspect is the direction of slope, and the amount of radiant energy reaching the land is influenced by this. A south-facing slope, for example, will receive more sun than a north-facing slope, and therefore have a generally warmer, drier soil and more abundant plant growth. Frost and snow will tend to persist for a shorter period of time.

The altitude is the height of the land above sea-level. Low ground and valleys tend to suffer less exposure to wind than hills and high ground.

A record of these topographical factors, a sketch map and a list of the main grasses present for an area, are a useful starting point for any exercise, and are of value in future discussion.

Identification of grasses presents a variety of problems. Mowing, trampling and grazing very often leave plants without leaf tips and flower heads, so that whole grass plants are difficult to find. Searching close to hedges, fences and walls for plants that are likely still to be intact, may bias the results, as these may be species less typical of the whole area. If areas are sought where the pressures of mowing, trampling or grazing are less, certain species may dominate to the exclusion of others. Thus grasses for initial identification should be selected from a representative region of the study area. More accurate identification can be achieved by allowing species to develop fully either by sectioning off an area from grazing, mowing or trampling, or by transplanting small pieces of turf to an area free of these pressures.

For identification, a key to some of the most common grasses follows this exercise. To identify a specimen, read the first couplet and decide which choice applies. Then follow the key through until you reach the final identification. Details should be checked with a hand lens although all characteristics used in the key can be seen with the naked eye. For all species vegetative characteristics are used, and for some, details of the flowering spike are included as well.

Exercise 1: to describe a grassland site

Materials

Notebook and pencil; Ordnance Survey map of the study area; scale 1:50 000; Ordnance Survey geological map; hand lens ($\times 10$); compass; clinometer; key to some of the most common grasses.

Time

1 h.

Method

(a) Record the grid reference of the site using the Ordnance Survey map, so that the study area may be readily located.
(b) Prepare a fully labelled sketch plan of the area. On your plan record the following information:

   (i) dimensions (approximate); (ii) aspect, using a compass; (iii) gradient, using a clinometer; (iv) altitude, using an OS map; (v) topography, using an OS map and field observations; (vi) bedrock, using an OS geological map; (vii) boundaries present, e.g. fences, roads; (viii) environmental pressures maintaining the grassland, e.g. grazing by sheep, mowing; (ix) prominent landmarks, e.g. posts, thickets.

(c) Identify the dominant grass species using the key to some of the most common grasses.

Questions

(1) Suggest the effects the following might have on the vegetation:
   (i) aspect; (ii) gradient; (iii) areas bordering the grassland; (iv) bedrock.
(2) What factors other than those measured might be influencing the vegetation?
(3) Which species appear to be common in the study area? Relate these to the factor(s) maintaining the grassland.

Key 1: to some of the most common grasses

Glossary (see Fig 1a)

sheath   The lower part of a leaf surrounding the stem.
ligule   A small flap of tissue on a leaf surface where the leaf separates from the stem (see Fig. 1b).
node   The point on the stem from where a leaf bract arises.
internode   The distance between nodes.
auricle   A small claw or ear-like growth at the junction of sheath and a blade of grass.
blade   The portion of a leaf above the sheath.

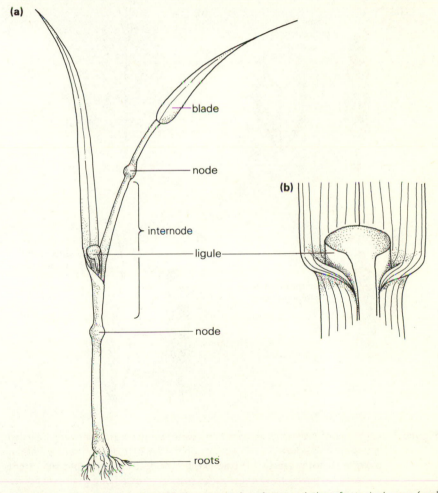

Figure I   Diagrams to show (a) the vegetative characteristics of a typical grass (scale ×0), and (b) an enlargement of the ligule.

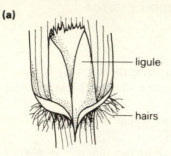

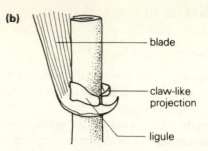

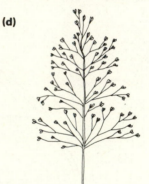

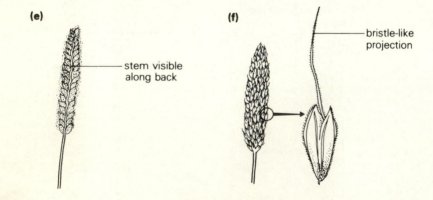

Figure 2 (a) Ligule of *Anthoxanthum odoratum* (sweet vernal grass), showing bearded appearance; (b) claw-like projections on the ligule; (c) flower head of *Phleum pratense* (timothy grass); (d) tree-like flower heads as in *Agrostis spp*. (bent grasses); (e) flower head of *Cynosurus cristatus* (crested dog's tail); (f) flower head of *Alopecurus pratensis* (meadow or common fox-tail).

Key

1   Ligule a dense fringe of short hairs.

(purple moor grass) *Molinia caerulea*

Ligule membranous.   **2**

2   Forming large tussocks. Leaves coarse and stiff, feeling like
rough sandpaper to touch.   (tufted hair grass) *Deschampsia caespitosa*

Not as above.   **3**

3   Fine, hairless long-leaved grasses. Leaves usually rolled to
give a hair or soft bristle-like appearance. Ligule very short,
usually <0.5 mm.   (red fescue) *Festuca rubra*

or (sheep's fescue) *Festuca ovina*

Not as above.   **4**

4   Leaves and stem densely covered in fine hairs. Very soft to
touch.   **5**

Leaves with some hairs or hairless. Smooth or slightly rough
to touch.   **6**

5   Ligule 1–4 mm. Nodes downy. Stem bases sometimes pink or
mauve. Leaves very soft.   (Yorkshire fog) *Holcus lanatus*

Ligule toothed, up to 2.5 mm long. Nodes with short hairs.
Upper leaves sometimes hairless.

(soft brome) *Bromus hordeaceus (B. mollis)*

6   Hair tufts at sheath apex giving area around ligule a bearded
appearance (Fig. 2a). Distinct scent when crushed. Often
quite hairy.   (sweet vernal grass) *Anthoxanthum odoratum*

Not as above.   **7**

7   Hook or claw-like outgrowths at junction of sheath and blade.
Stem bases may be very pink-red.   **8**

Not as above.   **9**

8   Hairless glossy leaves. Stem bases pink-red. Ligule 2 mm.
Small, narrow claw-like projections on leaves at junction of
leaves with ligule (Fig. 2b).   (rye grass) *Lolium perenne*

Leaves dull green, rather coarse, sometimes with scattered
hairs. Ligule very small, 1 mm long. Short auricles with small
projections. Sometimes tufted or spreading extensively.

(couch grass) *Elymus repens (Agropyron repens)*

9   Stem, leaves or both, strongly flattened.   **10**

Not as above.   **11**

10 Bluish-green, coarse, often robust grass. Leaves flattened to
give a keeled appearance. Stems especially flattened.

(cock's foot) *Dactylis glomerata*

Green leaves with hood-like tips giving a boat-like
appearance. Leaves often crinkled when young.

(meadow grasses) *Poa* **spp.**

11   Coarse, long-leaved grass, blades loosely hairy. Roots
     yellowish.   (false oat grass) *Arrhenatherum elatius*
     Leaves hairless.   **12**

N.B.   Throughout the rest of the key, details of flowering spikes are included, but it is
still possible to identify plants lacking spikes.

12   Shoot base bulbous. Ligule pointed. Each unit of the flower
     head with two bristle-like projections (awns) (Fig. 2c).
                                         (Timothy grass) *Phleum pratense*
     Shoot base not swollen.   **13**
13   Plant strongly decumbent. Leaf blades very pointed. Flower
     heads tree-like (Fig. 2d).   **14**
     Not as above.   **15**
14   Ligule shorter than broad. Stems mainly upright.
                                         (common bent) *Agrostis tenuis*
     Ligule up to 6 mm. Stems mainly decumbent, appearing
     distinctly jointed.   (creeping bent) *Agrostis stolonifera*
15   Ligules very blunt. Leaf sheaths yellow. Leaves bright
     yellow–green. Flower head one-sided, with stem visible along
     the back (Fig. 2e).   (crested dog's tail) *Cynosurus cristatus*
     Old sheaths dark brown. Ligule up to 6 mm, blunt. Each unit
     of the flower head with a single bristle-like projection
     (Fig. 2f).   (meadow or common fox-tail) *Alopecurus pratensis*

Vegetation analysis

Background

The vegetation is fundamental to the ecology of grasslands. It provides a habitat for a whole range of organisms, and the composition of the sward determines the characteristic appearance of different grasslands (e.g. lawns, meadows and cricket pitches). Vegetation cover and the action of plant roots in the soil help to maintain stability and prevent soil erosion.

The exercises in this section begin by introducing both qualitative and quantitative vegetation-sampling techniques with particular reference to the grassland ecosystem (Exercises 2–4). They then go on to investigate factors that are more directly related to grasslands, including grazing, trampling and mowing. The fact that the vegetation is held in check by the factors just mentioned is discussed in Exercise 8, where succession is considered. All of the exercises in this section can be linked with the other sections in this book (see Introduction).

The problems of identification of grassland species are discussed in Exercise 1, which is followed by a key to some of the most common grasses. This section contains illustrations of some of the most common grassland flowers. These are obviously not going to cover the whole range of species encountered, so the Bibliography lists several books which contain excellent illustrations and photographs of flowers, as well as keys.

Exercise 2: the listing of species and use of an abundance scale

Background

A list of the plant species present in the study area is a useful starting point for a description of the vegetation. The list by itself is only of limited value, but when combined with a subjective assessment of the relative abundance of the various species, then a clearer picture of the study area emerges.

A subjective assessment of abundance is given by the DAFOR scale where

D = dominant,
A = abundant,
F = frequent,
O = occasional,
R = rare.

As a general guide to using this scale, a species would be rated as dominant if it covered most or all of an area. An abundant species would be encountered often and cover between about a half and three-quarters of an area. If a species were frequent, it would be well scattered throughout a site, but certainly cover less than half the area. An occasional species occurs just a few times, and a rare one only once or twice.

The scale does however present certain problems which are listed below:

(a)   small species are often under-assessed;
(b)   conspicuous species are often over-assessed;
(c)   identification needs to be accurate;
(d)   vegetation changes with the time of year;
(e)   assessment is subjective;
(f)   an individual worker will assess vegetation more consistently than a group.

The following exercise will help with the other exercises in this book and should form part of the preliminary survey of any site under investigation.

N.B.   Guides for identification other than those provided are listed in the Bibliography. If some species cannot be readily identified they can be given a name such as 'X' or 'Y' or 'dandelion type' along with a brief description and sketch.

Aim

To list species and assess abundance using the DAFOR scale for a grassland site.

Materials

Key to some of the most common grasses; illustrations of some common grassland flowers (Fig. 3); 4 × 10-m tapes; ×10 hand lens

Time

1 h.

Method

(a)   Use the four tapes to form a 10 × 10 m square.
(b)   Within this area, identify the grasses and flowers using the grasses key and flower illustrations.
(c)   Assess the abundance of each species on the DAFOR scale by walking across the square.

Ranunculus repens, creeping buttercup
RANUNCULACEAE

Perennial, height up to 60 cm; yellow flowers and three-lobed hairy leaves; spreading with runners.

Common throughout Britain. *R. acris* (meadow buttercup) and *R. bulbosus* (bulbous buttercup) are also common in grasslands

Lotus corniculatus, bird's foot trefoil
LEGUMINOSAE

Perennial, height up to 35 cm; yellow flowers streaked with red, especially when in bud; stems solid, usually hairless; leaves made up of five leaflets

Trifolium dubium, lesser hop trefoil
LEGUMINOSAE

Annual, height up to 10 cm; 10–20 yellow flowers per flower head; trailing stems; leaves made up of three leaflets

Trifolium repens, white/Dutch clover
LEGUMINOSAE

Perennial, height up to 25 cm; white flowers; leaves made up of three leaflets; creeping and rooting at the nodes

Heracleum sphondylium, hogweed
UMBELLIFERAE

Biennial, height up to 200 cm; white or pinkish notched unequal petals; stems hollow, rigid and hairy; leaves rough, coarse-toothed and clasping the stem

Flower

Seed head

Figure 3   Illustrations of some common grassland flowers.

(d)   Convert the DAFOR scale to a numerical scale, i.e.

D = 5
A = 4
F = 3
O = 2
R = 1

and plot a bar chart showing the abundance of each species.

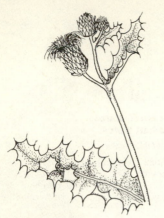

**Cirsium arvense,
creeping thistle**

COMPOSITAE

Perennial, height up to 100 cm; flowers
mauve or occasionally white, in clusters;
stems spineless, furrowed, unwinged;
leaves wavy and toothed with spiney
edges. *C. vulgare* (spear thistle) is also
common in grasslands

**Plantago lanceolata,
ribwort plantain**

Perennial, height up to 40 cm; flowers
much reduced with long white stamens;
leaves with strong parallel veins,
forming a basal rosette

**Taraxacum officinale (agg.),
dandelion**

COMPOSITAE

Yellow flowers with unbranched hollow
stems; leaves toothed or lobed,
forming a basal rosette

**Hypochaeris radicata,
cat's ear**

COMPOSITAE

Perennial, height up to 40 cm; yellow
flowers with outer petals greyish
beneath; stems usually hairless, and
forked, with scale-like bracts towards
the top; leaves covered in simple hairs,
forming a basal rosette

Figure 3 continued

Questions

(1) Which species predominate in the study area? Suggest reasons for their
success.

(2) What problems were encountered when assessing different species
using the abundance scale?

Veronica chamaedrys, germander speedwell

SCROPHULARIACEAE

Perennial, height up to 40 cm; flowers bright blue with a white centre; stems with two opposite rows of long white hairs; leaves hairy, toothed and usually stalkless

Bellis perennis, daisy

COMPOSITAE

Perennnial, height up to 8 cm; white outer (ray) florets, yellow inner (disc) florets; leaves basal, forming a rosette, slightly fleshy; stem has no leaves and is hairy

Senecio jacobaea, ragwort

COMPOSITAE

Biennial or perennial, height up to 150 cm; yellow flowers and furrowed leafy stems; basal leaves forming a rosette; stem leaves with blunt terminal lobes

Figure 3   continued

(3)   Suggest ways of overcoming some of the problems discussed in 2.
(4)   How might you use the abundance scale to compare the vegetation of two or more grassland sites?

Exercise 3: the determination of optimum quadrat size

Background

The most accurate way to obtain quantitative information about the plants and animals on a particular site is to record every individual on the whole site. This is clearly impractical except for very small areas, so we take samples, usually by selecting small parts of the site for intensive study. A quadrat is a sample area of defined size and shape and it is assumed that the contents of the quadrat will be representative of the whole site.

The size and number of quadrats employed will depend on the object of the study and on the nature of the vegetation or animals in the study area. A very small quadrat will only record a proportion of the species present so many quadrat samples will be required to build up a detailed and accurate picture of the site, whereas too large a quadrat (the largest possible quadrat would, of course, cover the whole site) will require an unnecessary amount of recording. Where the aim of the study is to determine the species composition of the site, the optimum quadrat size can be described as the size below which the number of different species found in the quadrat depends strongly on its area and above which the number of species found is relatively independent of area. It is a point beyond which there is a diminishing return of new information for increasing recording effort. Exercise 3 gives a method for determining this size. The number of quadrats used depends mainly on the level of accuracy required and is given for all exercises here.

Aim

To determine the optimum size of quadrat required to sample any area of grassland.

Materials

3 tapes (10 or 30 m); 2 × 2-m lengths of cord with skewers or pegs at each end; key to some of the most common grasses; illustrations of some common grassland flowers (Fig. 3).

Time

1 h.

Method

(a) Select a point in the study area.
(b) Place two tapes at right angles to each other and unroll about 2 m of each.
(c) Secure one end of each cord at the 0.1 m marks on each tape. Pull the cords taut to form a 0.1 × 0.1 m square with the tapes and secure them (Fig. 4). Angles can be checked by application of Pythagoras' theorem.
(d) Identify and record the species present within the square.
(e) Move the cords to the 0.2 m marks on the tapes to form a 0.2 × 0.2 m square.
(f) Search for and record any additional species.
(g) Repeat this procedure about ten times.
(h) Plot a graph of quadrat area against the number of species recorded in it.

Table 1 and Fig. 5 show the results obtained for two different grasslands. Site 1 is an uncut field and site 2 is a lawn.

Questions

(1) What reasons can be suggested for the difference in optimum quadrat size between sites 1 and 2?

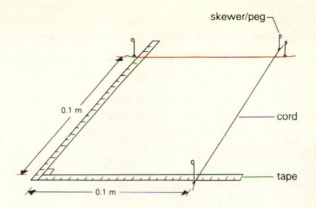

Figure 4 To show the arrangement of tapes and cords to form quadrats

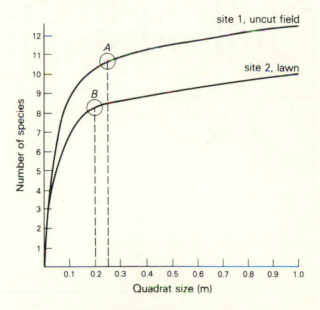

Figure 5 This shows that the optimum quadrat size for site 1 can be found at about A (which gives a size of about 0.2 m) whereas for site 2 it is at B (which gives a size of about 0.25 m).

(2) List some of the advantages and disadvantages of using a quadrat larger than the determined optimum.

(3) What effect will the dispersion, i.e. the way individuals are arranged in space, have on the size of the quadrat used?

Table 1 Table of results for numbers of species in relation to quadrat size for an uncut field (site 1) and a lawn (site 2); × indicates the presence of a species.

Site 1 : uncut field

Species	\ Quadrat size (m)									
	0.1	0.2	0.3	0.4	0.5	0.6	0.7	0.8	0.9	1.0
Trifolium repens white clover	×	×	×	×	×	×	×	×	×	×
Holcus lanatus Yorkshire fog	×	×	×	×	×	×	×	×	×	×
Plantago lanceolata ribwort plantation		×	×	×	×	×	×	×	×	×
Anthoxanthum odoratum sweet vernal grass		×	×	×	×	×	×	×	×	×
Veronica chamaedrys germander speedwell		×	×	×	×	×	×	×	×	×
Agrostis tenuis common bent			×	×	×	×	×	×	×	×
Rumex acetosa sorrel			×	×	×	×	×	×	×	×
Festuca rubra red fescue			×	×	×	×	×	×	×	×
Potentilla reptans creeping cinquefoil				×	×	×	×	×	×	×
Agrostis stolonifera creeping bent				×	×	×	×	×	×	×
Glechoma hederacea ground ivy							×	×	×	×
Arrhenatherum elatius oat grass										×
TOTAL NO. OF SPECIES	2	5	8	10	10	10	11	11	11	12

Site 2: lawn

Species	\ Quadrat size (m)									
	0.1	0.2	0.3	0.4	0.5	0.6	0.7	0.8	0.9	1.0
Trifolium repens white clover	×	×	×	×	×	×	×	×	×	×
Poa annua annual poa	×	×	×	×	×	×	×	×	×	×
Agrostis stolonifera creeping bent	×	×	×	×	×	×	×	×	×	×
Bellis perennis daisy	×	×	×	×	×	×	×	×	×	×
Taraxacum officinale dandelion			×	×	×	×	×	×	×	×
Rumex acetosa sorrel			×	×	×	×	×	×	×	×
Leontodon autumnalis autumnal hawkbit			×	×	×	×	×	×	×	×
Dactylis glomerata cock's foot grass					×	×	×	×	×	×
Holcus lanatus Yorkshire fog									×	×
Plantago lanceolata ribwort plantation										×
TOTAL NO. OF SPECIES	4	4	7	7	8	8	8	8	9	10

Exercise 4: percentage cover and frequency of species

Background

Abundance.   So far, abundance has been assessed qualitatively using the DAFOR scale. To measure variations and changes in abundance between species and sites, a quantitative method is necessary. There are four main measurements of abundance: density, cover, frequency and biomass.

density   The number of individuals per unit area. An objective measure, but all individuals of the same species count as equal, and it is often difficult to identify individual plants.
cover   The amount or percentage of the ground covered by a species. Only really valuable as a means of assessing abundance for species with greater than 10% cover.
frequency   The number or percentage of sites in which a species occurs. Easily and rapidly assessed and gives an indication of the dispersion or arrangement of species within an area.
biomass   The dry mass of vegetation or animals at a given moment. Can be time-consuming to sort, dry and weigh individuals but biomass is a reliable measure of abundance.

Exercise 4 describes how cover and frequency can be studied.

Sampling.   It is impossible to assess a whole study area for abundance, and sampling is therefore necessary. Sampling sites should be located at random to eliminate possible bias. A random sample is obtained when each sampling site has the same probability of being chosen as any other.

Aim

To determine the percentage cover and frequency of species for a grassland site using randomly placed quadrats.

Materials

Two 30-m tapes; quadrat, 0.5×0.5 m, divided into 25 equal units (see Fig. 6); 40 sets of four-figure random numbers from 00 to 30.

Time

5 min to set tapes; 10 min per quadrat.

Method

(a)   Place the two tapes at right angles to each other to act as axes in the area to be studied.

(b) Locate each quadrat site by pacing, using the random numbers as *x* and *y* co-ordinates. For consistency always place the bottom left-hand corner of the quadrat where the co-ordinates meet (Fig. 6).

(c) Identify all species using the key to some of the most common grasses and the drawings of flowering plants, and estimate the percentage cover in the quadrat. Each 10 × 10 cm square equals 4%. Use these squares to help assess cover.

> N.B. Each species in a quadrat can have a theoretical maximum cover of 100%; therefore total percentage cover per quadrat may be greater than 100%. Record moss as 'moss'. If dead leaves, twigs, etc. or bare ground are present, record as 'litter' and 'bare ground' respectively.

(d) Record species with less than 1% cover as present (+).

(e) Repeat steps (b) to (d) using successive sets of random numbers for each quadrat. Repeat for 40 quadrats altogether.

(f) Record data in the following way:

	Random co-ordinates		
	03	00	04
Species	07	02	07
Agrostis tenuis	75%	80%	80%
Holcus lanatus	50%	10%	2%
Lolium perenne	25%	15%	
Bellis perennis	1%	2%	1%

(g) In order to obtain an average percentage cover figure for each species, add up all the percentages for a species and divide by the number of quadrats.

(h) Rank the species according to cover, with the highest first.

(i) Calculate percentage frequency for each species using the following formula:

$$\frac{\text{number of quadrats in which a species is found (frequency)}}{\text{number of quadrats}} \times 100$$

(j) Plot bar graphs of average percentage cover and percentage frequency.

Questions

(1) Which species predominate in the study area in terms of percentage cover?

(2) Suggest reasons why the dominant species are so successful.

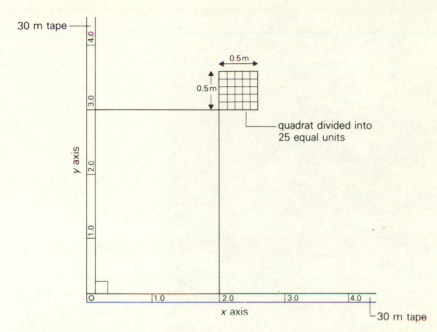

Figure 6 Diagram to show the location of a quadrat for random co-ordinates 0203.

(3) Discuss differences between results for percentage cover and fre-
     quency.
(4) What do these differences suggest about species dispersion?
(5) Design an experiment to compare two contrasting grasslands using
     either percentage cover or frequency as a measure of abundance.

Exercise 5: a comparison of a trampled and an untrampled area

Background

Each time a cow walks across a field, or a person walks along a path, they are
having a marked effect on the vegetation. Trampling damages plant shoots
and compresses the soil. Soil compaction impedes drainage and causes pools
of water to form in wet weather. Species that survive in trampled areas often
have special morphological adaptations to resist these effects. Daisies (*Bellis
perennis*), cat's ear (*Hypochaeris radicata*) and ribwort plantain (*Plantago
lanceolata*), for example, have rosette growth forms (Fig. 7a, and 12a).
Some species such as creeping bent grass (*Agrostis stolonifera*) and the
creeping buttercup (*Ranunculus repens*), spread along the soil surface producing mat forms (see illustration of *R. repens*; Fig. 3).

Figure 7 Rosette growth forms: (a) daisy (*Bellis perennis*); (b) cat's ear (*Hypochaeris radicata*) in an exposed grassland (see Fig. 12); (c, *right*) this shows an example of the type of area suitable for this exercise.

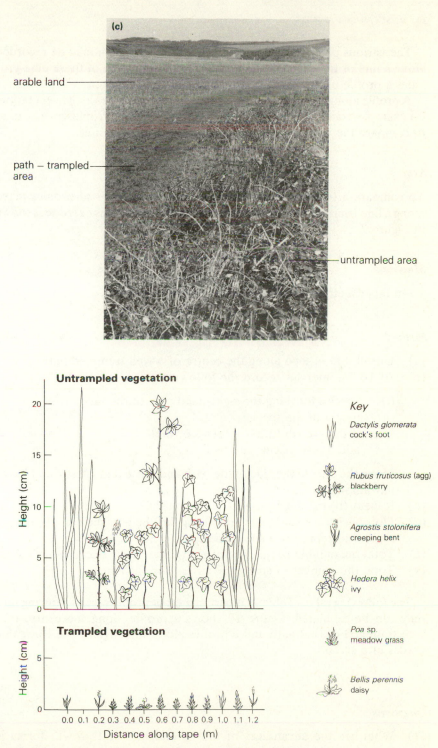

Figure 8 Profiles of the vegetation in the trampled and an untrampled area.

The various plant species, together with their heights, may be recorded along a line or transect. A semi-pictorial reconstruction of these data provides a profile of the vegetation (see Fig. 8).

A profile along a transect is useful in that it reveals zones in the vegetation, for example, transition from a grassland to a woodland. Profiles may be used to compare the vegetation of two or more contrasting sites.

Aim

To compare a trampled and untrampled area by means of profiles taken along a line transect. An example of a suitable area for this exercise is shown in Figure 7c.

Materials	Time
10-m tape; metre rule; identification guides.	1 h.

Method

(a)   Unroll 4 m of tape along the centre of a well trampled path.

(b)   At 10-cm intervals record the following:

     (i)   species touching the right-hand side of the tape;

     (ii)   height of the species;

     (iii) if the growth form is rosette or mat;

     (iv) additional species nearby.

(c)   Move the tape to the side of the path and place it in a less trampled or untrampled area.

(d)   Repeat (b) for this transect.

(e)   Plot species at each 10-cm interval against height (see Fig. 10) using a symbol to represent each species.

(f)   Total the number of times rosette and mat plants occur in each area.

(g)   Total the number of species recorded for each area.

The following table (Table 2) is part of a set of profile results showing how they can be tabulated. Figure 10 shows a profile along the centre of a well-trampled coastal path and a profile along the edge of the track that grades into scrub.

Questions

(1)   What are the advantages of the rosette and mat growth forms in trampled areas?

Table 2 An example of the tabulation of profile results.

Distance along tape (m)	Species	Species height (cm)	Rosette form	Mat form	Notes
0.0	Dactylis glomerata	1.0			
0.1	bare earth	–			Dactylis glomerata, flat clump nearby
0.2	Agrostis stolonifera	1.0		×	
0.3	Poa annua	0.5			Agrostis stolonifera nearby
0.4	Poa annua	1.0			
0.5	Bellis perennis	1.0	×		
0.6	Poa annua	1.5			

(2) Which of the two areas has the most species? Suggest reasons for any difference.

(3) What might be influencing the height of the vegetation in the absence of trampling?

(4) Find out how grasses grow. Why are they successful in trampled areas?

(5) Find out how the trampled area is maintained, i.e. is it trampled by animals or humans?

(6) List other factors that could be measured in the trampled areas. Use other exercises in this book as a basis for testing some of your ideas in a trampled and an untrampled area.

(7) The change in the height of the ground can also be measured along the transect. See Exercise 8 for details and adapt them for this exercise. How might the shape of the land affect the vegetation in (a) trampled and (b) untrampled areas? (See Exercise 1).

(8) Design an experiment to study the effects of (i) light, and (ii) heavy, trampling by humans.

Exercise 6: the effects of mowing

Background

Grazing by sheep, cattle and rabbits is a major factor in maintaining grass-land vegetation and determining species composition. Different animals tend to have different methods of grazing. For example, cows tend to tear the vegetation, gripping it with the tongue and hard pad of the upper jaw, whereas sheep and rabbits nibble with incisor teeth and can crop the veg-etation much shorter than cattle. These animals are selective in what they eat, having a preference for succulent species and tending to avoid prickly, hairy or tough woody species. Some plants in grassland are distasteful and may be poisonous, for example ragwort (*Senecio jacobaea*). These weeds are therefore not subject to the same grazing pressure and tend to thrive.

Mowing has a similar effect to animal grazing, but unlike grazing it is non-selective and can cut the vegetation uniformly close. At the same time it minimises the effects of trampling which complicates the direct effects on the vegetation of grazing animals.

The effects of non-selective grazing can therefore be studied by setting up different mowing regimes as described in this exercise.

A point quadrat is used to record changes in the vegetation (see Fig. 9a). This consists of a frame, usually with ten evenly-spaced holes supported by legs. A pin is dropped down on to the vegetation and each species hit by the tip of the pin recorded (see Fig. 9b).

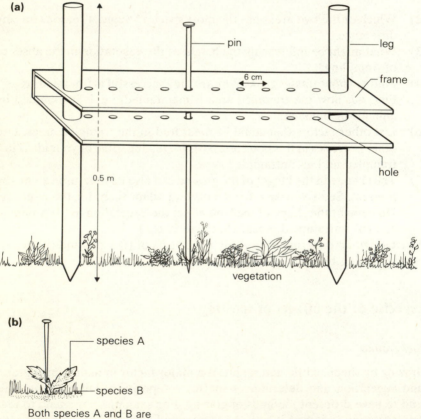

Both species A and B are
hit by the pin.
Both are recorded.

Figure 9 The point quadrat.

This method determines the presence or absence of species. The vegetation struck by the tip of the pin constitutes the area studied, and is equivalent to a very small quadrat. By using the point quadrat a rapid, objective assessment of vegetation cover is obtained, unlike assessment of cover with a frame quadrat (see Exercises 3 and 4) where it is subjective.

Aim

To study the effects of mowing in a series of grassland plots over a period of time.

Materials

Lawn mower; fencing; metre rule; point quadrat; 40 sets of four-figure random numbers from 00 to 29 for the x axis and from 00 to 25 for the y axis.

Time

At least six months; 45 min to monitor each plot.

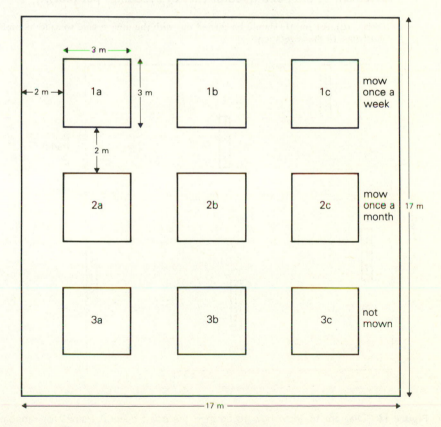

Figure 10 Diagram to show the arrangement of plots.

Method

(a) At the start of the growing season (about April) fence off an area of grassland, for example part of a cricket field or lawn, 17 × 17 m.

(b) Within this area mark out nine plots, 3 × 3 m, leaving 2 m between each plot and a 2-m band around the edge (see Fig 10).

(c) Mow plots 1a, b and c once a week; mow plots 2a, b and c once a month; leave plots 3a, b and c unmown.

(d) Monitor the vegetation once a week, placing the quadrat frame five times in each plot using the random co-ordinates. Figure 11 shows how to locate and position the quadrats for five sets of random numbers. (See also Exercise 4 for information on random co-ordinates.)

(e) Record each species the pin hits for each hole of the point quadrat. If the same species is hit more than once for one pin drop, it only counts as one hit, i.e. the maximum number of times a species can theoretically be hit for each plot is 50 times (100% cover).

(f) Measure the height of the tallest piece of vegetation found for each placement of the point quadrat (i.e. five readings per plot).

> N.B.   (d), (e) and (f) should be carried out with the utmost care so as to minimise disturbance to the vegetation.

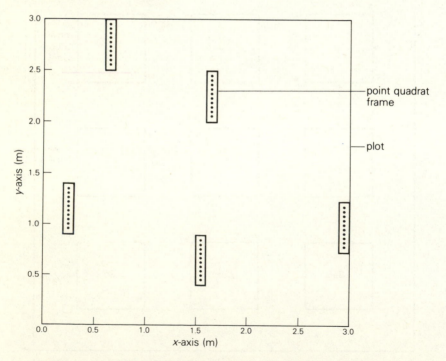

Figure 11   Diagram to show how to arrange the point quadrat frames for random co-ordinates 0209, 0625, 1504, 1620 and 2907.

(g) Convert the numbers for each species in each plot to a percentage cover as follows:

Let x = the number of hits per plot per species. For 50 drops of the pin, percentage cover is

$$\frac{x}{50} \times 100 = 2x$$

(h) Combine the weekly data to give an average percentage cover for each set of plots by adding up the three percentages for each species and dividing by three.

(i) Calculate the average tallest height of the vegetation for each set of plots by adding up the 15 readings and dividing by 15.

(j) Plot the average percentage cover of each species against time, for each set of plots.

(k) Plot the average tallest height of the vegetation against time, for each set of plots.

(l) List the following for each set of plots:

  (i)   species that have decreased in number;
  (ii) species that have increased in number;
  (iii) new species;
  (iv) species that show no obvious pattern;
  (v)   species that have remained relatively constant.

Questions

(1) Describe briefly, for each set of plots, the changes in species composition and vegetation height which have occurred over the period of the investigation.

(2) Suggest reasons for recorded changes in individual species. Can these be related in any way to the shape of the plant concerned? (See Exercise 5).

(3) What effect might any changes be having on the soil? Design an experiment(s) to measure some of these possible effects. Use Exercises 13, 16–18 and 21–26 to help provide ideas.

(4) Biomass is the mass of living material. Outline how the biomass of the vegetation of each set of plots could be harvested, dried and weighed to compare changes over a period of time. How might the kind of information obtained from such a study be of use to a farmer?

(5) Predict what changes might occur to the vegetation in each set of plots, over the next few years, if the exercise were extended. (See Exercise 8 on succession.)

(6) Comment on the use of the point quadrat. Can you suggest reasons for using a point quadrat for this exercise, other than those given in the background information?

Exercise 7: species variation

Background

The results of Exercises 5 and 6 demonstrate that grazing, mowing and trampling not only modify the species composition of grasslands but also the morphology of the species. Variation is found in all plants and animals; it is determined by two factors:

The effect of the environment. Individuals of a species occurring in different habitats, will be subjected to different environmental stresses. For example, sea pink or thrift (*Armeria maritima*) and sea plantain (*Plantago maritima*) are found in both saltmarshes and exposed cliff grassland, and show considerable variation in form between the two habitats.

Genetic variability. The genetic structure of populations in different habitats tends to be different because members of a population that are well adapted to the environment will tend to outcompete those that are not so well suited, and this will influence characters such as morphology.

The following exercise studies variation between different sites; and uses the readily-available daisy (*Bellis perennis*), but there are many other species commonly occurring in different types of grassland that would be equally suitable, e.g. ribwort plantain (*Plantago lanceolata*), or cat's ear (*Hypochaeris radicata*). Figures 12a and b show ribwort plantain in short, exposed grassland (Fig. 12a) and in an uncut verge (Fig. 12b).

For this exercise choose two different habitats where daisies are common or abundant, for example a grassy, disused track grazed by horses, and a lawn.

Aim

To study the variation in stem length, leaf length and leaf width of *Bellis perennis* (daisy) in two different grasslands.

Materials

10-m tape; 15-cm rule; pair of callipers, graduated in 0.1 mm.

Time	Method
2 h.	Follow this procedure in both study areas.

Stems

(a) Unroll 5 m of tape along the study area.

(b) Select the flower closest to the first 10 cm of the tape (see Fig. 13a).

Figure 12 (a) Ribwort plantain (*Plantago lanceolata*), in short, exposed grassland. (Note daisies towards top left of plantain colony.); (b) Ribwort plantain in an uncut verge.

(c)   Measure the length of the stem using callipers.
(d)   Repeat for successive 10-cm lengths of tape until 50 stems have been measured.

Leaves
(e)   At 10-cm intervals along the tape, pick the first daisy leaf found along a line at right angles to the tape (see Fig. 13b).
(f)   Measure the length of the leaf from base to tip.
(g)   Measure the width of the leaf at the widest point.
(h)   Repeat until 50 leaves have been measured.
(i)   Group the values for stem length, leaf length and width into size classes for the two areas.
(j)   Plot histograms of size class against frequency.
(k)   Calculate the mean value for stem length, leaf length and leaf width.

Figure 14 shows the results of this exercise for stem length of daisies from the lawn and track.

Questions

(1)   Discuss the differences between the means of the leaf lengths, widths and stem lengths for the two sites, suggesting reasons for them.
(2)   Which graphs of each variable appear to show the greatest variation? Suggest reasons for this.
(3)   What other measurements might have revealed variation? Give reasons for your suggestions.
(4)   What statistical test could be used to see if the variation between sites was significant?
(5)   Choose another species on which to carry out a similar study, indicating which variables you would measure and why.

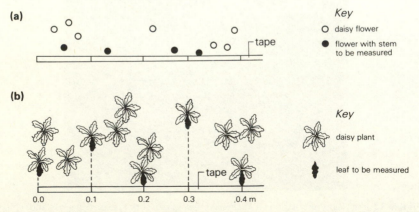

Figure 13   Diagrams to show (a) the selection of daisy stems to be measured; and (b) the selection of daisy leaves to be measured.

(a)

Size class (mm)	Numbers in each class (frequency)	
	Site 1	Site 2
0 – 9.9	1	0
10 – 19.9	6	15
20 – 29.9	11	13
30 – 39.9	14	19
40 – 49.9	7	2
50 – 59.9	8	1
60 – 69.9	2	0
70 – 79.9	1	0

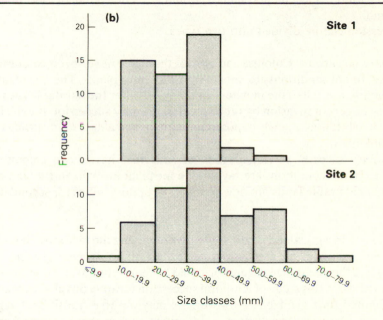
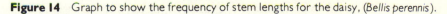

Figure 14   Graph to show the frequency of stem lengths for the daisy, (Bellis perennis).

Exercise 8: succession

Background

Have you ever gone into the garden in a fit of enthusiasm, tidied it, cleared the vegetable plot of weeds, cut the lawn, and then gone away for a few weeks? On return the result is only too apparent! The ground is once again full of weeds and the lawn is turning into a hay meadow. Left to themselves, the plants would alter the environment. The amount of living matter would increase as the vegetation grew, and this would affect the soil by providing more nutrients and organic matter, and increased shading. In time the more successful species may eliminate those less well adapted; they may also modify the habitat, permitting the establishment of new species. This change in species composition of the community over a period of time is called **succession** and, ultimately, a final (or stable) stage is reached which is known as the **climax**. The climax community is self-perpetuating and in balance with the available resources for as long as all external influences remain constant. In the case of grassland ecosystems, the natural vegetational development is prevented, largely owing to the activities of man (see Introduction). This **biotic climax** is created by grazing, mowing, cutting and ploughing of grasslands, instead of by the natural climatic or edaphic (soil) factors. If these influences were removed, it is thought that, for much of lowland Britain, the climatic climax would be some kind of deciduous woodland.

Succession can be divided into two types:

Primary succession. Colonisation of soils that have never been colonised before. Initial conditions are unfavourable for most plants. The first plants to colonise are called the pioneers and they will alter the habitat in such a way as to permit invasion by other species. Primary succession is evident in such habitats as a newly exposed sand dune, and a new road cutting or embankment.

Secondary succession. Colonisation of soils that have been colonised before. Initial conditions are favourable for plant growth. Burnt land or abandoned arable lands provide examples of opportunities for secondary succession.

Succession in a grassland is best studied by removing the factors maintaining it. For example, an area might be fenced off to exclude grazing or mowing and the changes in vegetation could be monitored over a number of years. In practice this study of temporal succession is rarely possible because of the limited time available. However, we may observe transitional vegetation zones between two distinct communities, such as those grading from the centre of a pond to peripheral dry grassland; or between grassland and woodland, as described below. These zones may reflect the changes observed through time at a single site but it is important to understand that this exercise does NOT record temporal succession as discussed in the background, merely a spatial progression which may or may not represent a successional sequence.

Aims

(1) To record changes in species composition from a grassland to a woodland using a continuous belt transect.
(2) To record changes in height of the ground at metre intervals.

Materials

0.5 × 0.5 m quadrat; 2 canes; 1-m rule; spirit level; light string or cord (heavy cord will sag unless supported by additional canes).

Time

1½ h.

Method

(a) Select a suitable area of grassland that grades into woodland.
(b) Lay a tape from the open grassland into the woodland.
(c) At every half-metre interval, place the frame quadrat by the tape (see Fig. 15).
(d) In each quadrat, identify the species using the keys and illustrations provided. Record the percentage cover of each species (see Exercise 4).
(e) To record tree canopy cover, look up and estimate what area of the sky is obscured by the trees in the region directly above the quadrat.
(f) To record the change in height of the ground, insert one cane at 0 m by the tape and the other at 1 m along the tape.

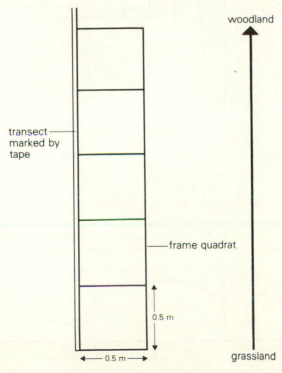

Figure 15 Diagram to show the placing of quadrats.

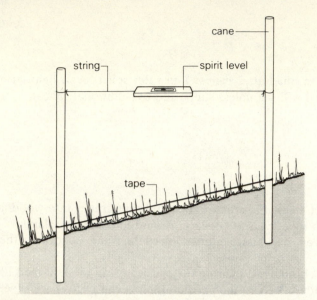

Figure 16 Diagram to show the arrangement of materials for a profile transect.

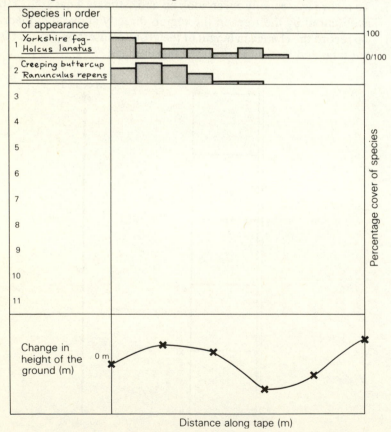

Figure 17 Graph to show how to plot the data obtained in Exercise 8.

(g)   Tie the string or cord to each cane to make a horizontal line about 0.5 m above the ground. Use the spirit level to check that the line is horizontal (see Fig. 16).

(h)   Measure the height of the string above the ground at 0 m and at 1 m. Record the difference. If the ground increases in height from the 0 to 1-m positions, record the difference as positive; if the ground decreases in height, record the difference as negative.

(i)   Plot a graph of change in height of the ground against distance along the tape. On the same graph plot percentage cover of each species at each sampling site (see Fig. 17).

Questions

(1)   Summarise the changes in the vegetation observed along the transect from the grassland to the woodland.

(2)   Discuss the change in percentage cover for each species along the transect.

(3)   Is there any evidence to suggest that competition between species is taking place?

(4)   Does the change in the shape of the ground (surface topography) appear to be having an effect on the vegetation, and what properties of the soil will it influence?

(5)   Suggest experiments to test the answers to question 4.

(6)   This exercise illustrates changes in plant communities through space. Design an experiment to study changes in plant communities with time, or succession.

Animal analysis

Background

Grasslands provide a range of habitats for animals both above and below the ground. Above the ground plants' flowers are visited by insects, for example butterflies, hover flies and bees, and succulent stems can provide food for insects with piercing mouthparts such as frog-hoppers (e.g. *Philaenus spumarius*) and aphids. Some species including grasshoppers, and butterflies of the Satyridae family (e.g. meadow brown butterfly), feed almost entirely on grass. Long grass provides cover for small mammals, especially voles, which in turn provide food for predators (see Exercise 15).

In the soil there is a whole range of other animals, avoiding the problems of desiccation that face those living on the surface. Some feed on organic matter and play a very important part in the decomposition of dead remains (see p. 60).

Some animals cause economic damage and are therefore considered pests. These include some species of aphid above the ground, and leatherjackets below the ground.

There are certain problems associated with the study of animals. First, they are likely to have periods of activity (e.g. flying, running, jumping) which may follow diurnal rhythms such that the animal is only active at certain times – a nocturnal animal will only come out at night. When resting, animals may be difficult to find; plants, litter and soil all provide places of concealment. This means that a variety of techniques is required to catch or extract the animals. Secondly the problem of identification is severe. There are about 20 000 species of insect in Britain alone. To study and understand their ecology, however, it is not necessary to identify all of them to species level. Illustrations of some insect orders commonly found in grasslands (Fig. 19) and a key to some common soil organisms are provided (p. 52).

Exercise 9: a comparison of animals inhabiting long and short grass, using sweep nets, quadrats and pooters

Background

We require a variety of techniques in order to capture animals for study. A useful tool for animals which fly or crawl through the vegetation as well as

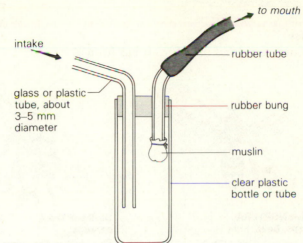

intake

to mouth

rubber tube

glass or plastic tube, about 3–5 mm diameter

rubber bung

muslin

clear plastic bottle or tube

Figure 18   The pooter.

those living or resting on plants is the sweep net. This is a strong net on a firm frame that is swept or dragged through the vegetation. Animals are then removed from the net with a pooter (which might be described as the ecologist's vacuum cleaner; see Fig. 18). This is a simple device whereby the ecologist sucks species through a tube into a collecting bottle.

One of the problems of using a sweep net to sample animals in long grass is that the animals may be difficult to dislodge from the plant bases. In short vegetation, also, many of the animals may be buried deep in the bases of the plants as a means of avoiding desiccation, which is a greater problem than for animals in the long grass. Another way of sampling the animals in the grass is by using a frame quadrat as used in the analysis of vegetation (see Exercise 3). Here the quadrat is systematically searched and any animals found collected in a pooter.

This exercise uses a combination of sweep netting and quadrats in order to obtain a wide range of the organisms present, as well as to compare the effectiveness of each technique.

Aim

To compare the animals collected from short and long grassland by (i) searching the area defined by a quadrat; and (ii) sweeping an area with a sweep net and removing animals using a pooter.

Materials

Four 10 m tapes; sweep net; pooter; collecting bottles; frame quadrat, 0.5 × 0.5 m, divided into 25 equal parts; ethanol; cotton wool; microscope; 8 sets of 4-figure random numbers between 00 and 10; labels.

Time
3 h.
Time of day
After the dew has dried or before it has formed.

Time of year
May–October.

HYMENOPTERA
wasps, bees, ants
Usually two pairs of wings with few veins; many have a narrow 'waist' between the thorax and abdomen

DERMAPTERA
earwigs
Short fore wings; pincers at the tail end; brownish colour

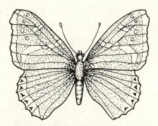

LEPIDOPTERA
butterflies and moths
Butterflies – antennae have club-shaped tips; moths – antennae never have club-shaped tips

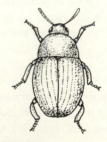

HEMIPTERA
bugs – includes aphids and froghoppers
Piercing mouthparts; two pairs of wings, with front pair often hardened

COLEOPTERA
beetles
Two pairs of wings, front pair hard, forming cases covering hind wings; biting mouthparts

Figure 19 Illustrations of some insect orders commonly found in grasslands.

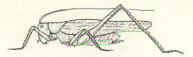

ORTHOPTERA
grasshoppers and crickets

Stout bodied and blunt headed; large hind legs; two pairs of wings usually with a thicker front pair

COLLEMBOLA
springtails

Wingless; often transparent and usually < 5 mm long; springing organ at the rear end

THYSANOPTERA
thrips

Dark with slim bodies; usually two pairs of narrow fringed wings; often found in flowers

DIPTERA
flies

One pair of wings; hind wings reduced to club-shaped balancers called halteres

Figure 19 continued

Method

For both sites:

(a) Mark out 2 areas 10 × 10 m, using the 10-m tapes.

(b) In one 10 × 10-m area, locate 8 quadrats randomly, using the method in Exercise 4.

(c) Search each quadrat thoroughly, working systematically through the 25 subdivisions.

(d) Pooter any animals found into a collecting bottle, and label.

(e) Sweep net the other 10 × 10-m area for 10 min. This should be carried out in the following way: sweep for one minute, then pooter all the animals in the net into a collecting bottle. Animals larger than the diameter of the pooter such as grasshoppers can be picked out by hand and put into a collecting bottle. Make sure that the stem bases and tips are both well swept. Repeat until 10 min has elapsed. Label all collecting bottles.

(f) Back in the laboratory, if necessary, inactivate the species by putting a little cotton wool soaked in ethanol in the collecting bottles.

(g) Sort and identify the animals to order or group. For the insects use Figure 19 to help with identification. You may need to use a microscope.

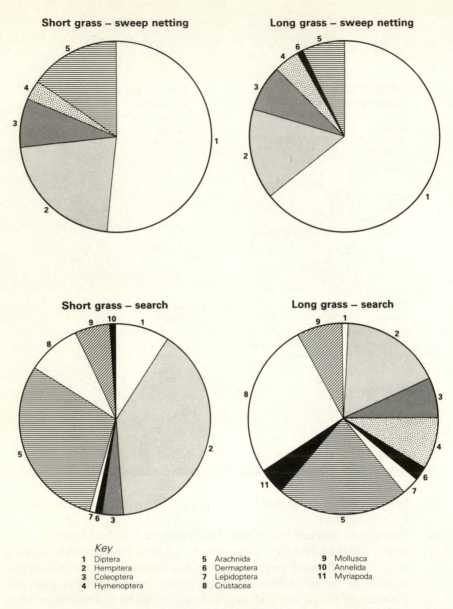

Short grass – sweep netting

Long grass – sweep netting

Short grass – search

Long grass – search

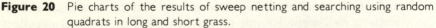

Key

1	Diptera	**5**	Arachnida	**9**	Mollusca
2	Hempitera	**6**	Dermaptera	**10**	Annelida
3	Coleoptera	**7**	Lepidoptera	**11**	Myriapoda
4	Hymenoptera	**8**	Crustacea		

Figure 20 Pie charts of the results of sweep netting and searching using random quadrats in long and short grass.

(h) Determine the number of each order or group for both sites and both sampling techniques.

(i) Display the data graphically in the form of pie charts for the orders and groups caught by searching and sweeping, for both sites. A pie chart is a visual representation of proportions and is a useful way to display data of the kind obtained in this exercise where numbers are not directly comparable. Construct the pie chart by converting the numbers obtained for each order or group to percentages and then multiplying by 3.6 to work out how many degrees of a circle each percentage represents. See the examples in Figure 20.

Questions

(1) Taking the results as a whole, suggest reasons for any differences observed between the animals caught in the long and short grass.

(2) What differences were there in the results obtained for (i) the sweep net at each site; and (ii) the quadrats at each site? Suggest reasons for these differences.

(3) What differences were there between the animals caught using the sweep nets and those collected from the quadrats, regardless of the vegetation?

(4) Comment on the use of the pooter. How effective is it in an exercise of this kind?

(5) List any problems encountered whilst sampling animals using the techniques described.

N.B. Return all undamaged animals to the grasslands at the end of the exercise.

Exercise 10: a study of ground invertebrate activity in a grassland

Background

At different times of the day and night some invertebrates are observed to be more active than others. Warmth from sunshine during the day will cause an increase in activity of sun-loving insects such as butterflies and hover flies. At the same time others may seek refuge from the drying and heating effects of the sun, perhaps in the cool moist bases of grass clumps where the micro-climate is more favourable. As well as avoiding desiccation, these organisms may be less visible to predators active in daytime. At night, when it is dark and humid, these invertebrates may emerge to forage for food.

By setting a series of pitfall traps, organisms moving through the veg-etation can be sampled over a period of time. A pitfall trap consists of any shallow container such as a jam jar which can be sunk into the soil with the opening at ground level. Traps can be set in a variety of ways, as illustrated in

Figure 21. If traps are to be left for longer than about 24 hours, 4% formalin should be substituted for the detergent to prevent specimens rotting.

As well as being a useful collecting device, pitfall traps can be used to study the activity of organisms with time.

Aim

To study the activity of invertebrates at ground level in a grassland by pitfall trapping over a 24-h period.

Materials

25 jars; trowel; 2 30-m tapes; forceps; microscope.

Time

24 h; 15 min to sort each trap.

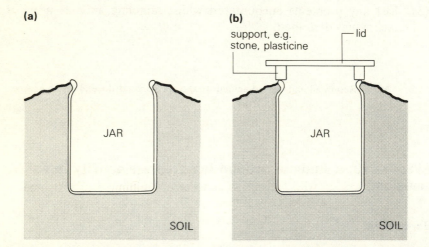

(a)

(b)

support, e.g. stone, plasticine — lid

JAR

JAR

SOIL

SOIL

Figure 21 (a) The basic trap: the jar is sunk into the ground with soil sloping away from the opening to prevent any drainage water flooding the trap. It is simple to set and easily emptied whilst in position, but has some disadvantages. Carnivorous species within the trap may eat other members of the catch and animals, such as frogs, may come to feed. Small mammals, for example mice, voles and shrews, risk falling in and being unable to escape. The trap is also subject to flooding by rain. The addition of water with a few drops of detergent solves the problem of damage to specimens caused by predation. (b) This figure shows a trap which is modified by having a lid, such as a tile or piece of wood, raised above the opening of the jar. The lid protects the trap from rain, larger predators and small mammals getting inside. It does not, however, overcome the problems of carnivores eating the catch.

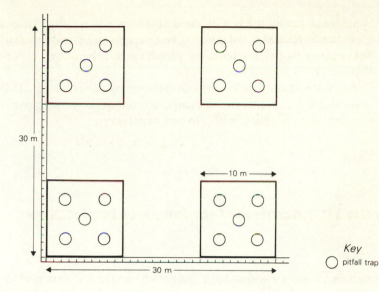

Figure 22 Diagram to show the arrangements of pitfall traps.

Method

(a) Mark out a square area 30 × 30 m in the grassland, using the tapes.

(b) At each corner make a square 10 × 10 m. In each of these subplots sink five jars, one in each corner and one in the middle (see Fig. 22). Try to disturb the area as little as possible.

(c) Make a note of the weather conditions.

(d) 4 h later, return and remove any organisms in the trap. This should be done carefully with forceps so as to create minimum disturbance.

(e) Note any change in the weather.

(f) Identify the catch to order or group and count the numbers in each.

(g) Repeat four more times.

(h) Return species to the study area after completion of the exercise.

(i) Plot the results for the numbers of individuals of different orders with time.

Questions

(1) Make a list of observations from the results of numbers of each order or group with time. Attempt some explanations of your findings.

(2) Do the weather observations appear to relate to any of the results obtained?

(3) How representative do you think numbers of individuals are in relation to total population size?

(4)   What do you think the results show about animal activity? Discuss the idea that 'catchability' of some species might influence the results.
(5)   Set up some baited and unbaited pitfall traps. Discuss any differences that occur.
(6)   Pitfall traps mainly catch organisms running or crawling along the ground. Devise an exercise to compare numbers of animals with time, for tops of grass plants with ground vegetation.

Exercise 11: comparison of the faunas of two localities

Background

The animals found in grassland are dependent on the habitats provided by the vegetation. Both the species present and the total number of organisms are related to the range of food and habitats available. Neutral grasslands, for example, tend to support a greater variety of plant species than acid grasslands and hence offer a larger number of habitats and a greater variety of food.

Exercise 11 illustrates a simple but effective way of studying organisms at two localities, using water traps. A water trap is any shallow dish or container half-filled with water plus a few drops of detergent. The detergent causes the organisms to sink. Empty ice cream or margarine tubs of the dimensions illustrated (see Fig. 23a) make very convenient traps. The surface area and colour of the trap may influence the catch.

Generally, the larger the surface area, the larger the catch. A very small area may be unprofitable in terms of the size of sample caught. Conversely, a very large dish may catch more organisms than can be identified in the time available. A reasonable trap surface area is between about 0.1 m² and 0.3 m².

Traps may be any colour. Certain colours, however, appear to be more effective than others at attracting certain types of organisms. White traps, for example, tend to attract members of the Diptera (flies), whereas yellow traps appear to catch aphids. The attractiveness of certain colours of trap would form the basis of an interesting project.

Water traps may be used in a variety of situations. They can be set simply to sample an area for its insect life, or to compare organisms at two or more localities. Relationships between catch and trap size or colour, or length and time of day of exposure can also be studied.

Examples of the types of comparison that could be made for this exercise are: uncut and cut grassland; exposed and sheltered grassland; grazed and ungrazed grassland; acid and neutral grassland; opposite ends of a field.

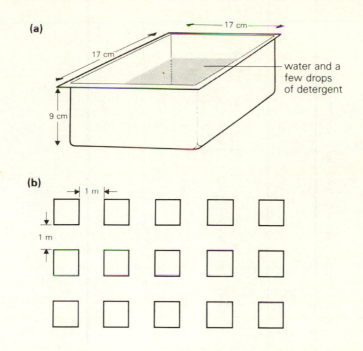

Figure 23   (a) Diagram of a water trap. (b) Diagram to show the arrangement of water traps.

Aim

To compare the faunas caught in water traps set over a 24-h period at two grassland localities.

Materials

30 water traps (these should be identical, but if this is not possible, a variety of traps can be used, provided that the same combination is used at each site, e.g. five round and ten square at each site); forceps; soft paintbrush; microscope; Petri dishes; identification aids (Fig. 19 and see Bibliography); water and detergent.

Time

24 h to leave traps, plus time to set and recover them; 45 min per trap for sorting.

Table 3 Data obtained from water traps set at two localities: site 1: short, exposed grass; and site 2: long, sheltered grass.

Trap number	Site 1											Site 2										
	1	2	3	4	5	6	7	8	9	10	Total	1	2	3	4	5	6	7	8	9	10	Total
Order/Group																						
Diptera	16	9	7	9	14	38	38	13	35	42	221	4	1	—	5	4	11	9	7	14	11	66
Hymenoptera	3	3	—	—	—	8	2	5	11	3	38	—	2	2	—	3	—	2	2	—	5	18
Coleoptera	1	2	—	2	—	11	2	—	14	10	42	1	—	—	—	—	2	2	1	—	—	7
Hemiptera	3	—	—	—	1	—	—	1	2	—	8	—	—	—	—	—	—	2	2	—	3	8
Collembola	—	—	—	—	—	—	—	—	—	—	—	—	—	—	—	13	—	—	—	—	—	14
Orthoptera	—	—	—	—	—	—	—	—	—	—	—	—	—	—	—	1	1	—	—	—	—	2
Trichoptera	—	—	—	—	—	—	—	—	2	—	2	—	—	—	—	—	—	—	—	—	—	—
Arachnida	1	—	—	1	—	—	—	1	1	—	4	—	2	—	—	—	—	—	1	1	—	4
Total	24	14	8	13	16	58	42	20	65	55	315	5	5	2	7	21	15	14	13	18	20	119

Method

(a) Select the two grassland localities to be studied.
(b) Place 15 traps systematically at 1-m intervals in five columns of three rows (see Fig. 23b).
(c) Half fill each trap with water and a few drops of detergent, and leave.
(d) 24 h later, collect the traps and sort each *separately* as follows:

    (i) Extract all individuals. Forceps and the paintbrush are useful for this exercise.

    (ii) Sort the animals into insect orders or other groups in Petri dishes.

    (iii) Record the number of *individuals* of each order or group in each trap.

Table 3 shows the results from ten white water traps set for 24 h at two grassland sites.

It is possible to see if there is a significant difference between the results for the two localities studied by applying the Mann–Whitney U test. This will reveal whether differences between the two sites in the numbers of a particular order or group are significant, or due merely to chance factors such as sampling error.

The Mann–Whitney U test

The worked example below is carried out on results for the Diptera (see Table 3), as members of this order are readily caught using water traps.

(a) The totals for each trap are put in ascending order for each site:
site 1: 7, 9, 9, 13, 14, 16, 35, 38, 38, 42.
site 2: 0, 1, 4, 4, 5, 7, 9, 11, 11, 14.

(b) The numbers for the two sites are then combined and put in ascending order, i.e. ranked – see line A. Each number is given a value related to its position in the rank, as shown in line B. Equal numbers are given average rank values – see line C.

A: 0, 1, 4, 4, 5, 7, 7, 9, 9, 9,   11, 11, 13, 14, 14, 16, 35, 38, 38, 42.
B: 1, 2, 3, 4, 5, 6, 7, 8, 9, 10, 11, 12, 13, 14, 15, 16, 17, 18, 19, 20.
C: 3½   6½   9   11½   14½   18½

The values for each site are then totalled, thus:

	Site 1			Site 2	
	7 ~	6½		0 ~	1
	9 ~	9		1 ~	2
	9 ~	9		4 ~	3½
	13 ~	13		4 ~	3½
	14 ~	14½		5 ~	5
	16 ~	16		7 ~	6½
	35 ~	17		9 ~	9
	38 ~	18½		11 ~	11½
	38 ~	18½		11 ~	11½
	42 ~	20		14 ~	14½
Totals		142			68

(c)   The values of U_1 and U_2 are then calculated:

$$U_1 = n_1 \times n_2 + \left[n_2 \frac{(n_2 + 1)}{2} \right] - R_2$$

where R_2 = the total for the rank of site 2, and n = the number in each sample, i.e.

$$10 \times 10 + \left[10 \frac{(10 + 1)}{2} \right] - 68$$

$$U_1 = 87$$

$$U_2 = n_1 \times n_2 + \left[n_1 \frac{(n_1 + 1)}{2} \right] - R_1$$

where R_1 = the total for the rank of site 1, i.e.

$$10 \times 10 + \left[10 \frac{(10 + 1)}{2} \right] - 142$$

$$U_2 = 13$$

(d)   The smallest calculated value of U is taken, and compared with the tabulated U statistic. In this example, U_2 has the smallest value, i.e. 13. The tabulated value for n_1 and $n_2 = 10$ is 23 at the 5% level of significance, i.e. for numbers less than 23 there is a 95% chance that the difference between the results is due to something other than chance. As U_2 is smaller than the tabulated value, the difference between the Diptera catches for the two localities is significant at the 5% level.

(e)   Apply the Mann–Whitney U test to some orders or groups.

Questions

(1) Suggest reasons why certain orders or groups have been caught and why some are more numerous than others. Relate this discussion to the vegetation present at each site.

(2) Comment on any bias that could have occurred in relation to the type of water trap used.

(3) Having applied the Mann–Whitney U test, try to give an explanation as to the significance of the results obtained.

(4) How may certain weather conditions affect the results?

(5) If you have encountered any problems in the method, list possible improvements.

(6) Suggest further studies that could be carried out to compare the two areas more closely for the faunas sampled by the water trap method.

Exercise 12: a study of organisms on flower heads

Background

During the summer months, many grassland plants come into flower. Certain species that are less succulent tend to be avoided by grazing animals (see Exercise 6). These include the prickly *Cirsium arvense* (creeping thistle) and *C. vulgare* (spear thistle), and the tough, fibrous *Heracleum sphondylium* (hogweed). If these species resist trampling effects as well (see Exercise 5) they will grow higher than the general level of the grassland sward. The flowers produced will provide a habitat for some organisms as well as nectar for visiting insects. These insects may in turn pollinate the flowers or may attract other predatory species. Some organisms may complete part or all of their life cycles in the heads of flowers.

This exercise lends itself to a range of other studies involving flower heads and animals associated with them. One particular species of insect could be studied over a period of time, or several flower species could be studied and compared. Other species that could be investigated include ragwort (*Senecio jacobaea*), spear thistle (*Cirsium vulgare*), and bramble (*Rubus fruticosus* (agg)). The types and numbers of insects visiting a particular flower head over a period of time could also be investigated.

Aim

To collect and record the organisms found on the flower heads of hogweed.

Materials	*Time*
Pooter; plastic bags; 30 canes; microscope.	2–3 h.

Method

(a) Locate an area of grassland containing hogweed.
(b) Carry out the following procedure for 30 plants:

    (i)   Select the top flower head. With as little disturbance as possible, cover the head with a plastic bag.
    (ii)   Shake the head to knock species into the plastic bag.
    (iii)   Remove the bag and close the top.
    (iv)   Check the flower head and pooter any species still attached.
    (v)   Pooter specimens from the plastic bag into a collecting tube.
    (vi)   Mark each plant studied with a cane.
    (vii)   Identify species to order or group and record the numbers of each.

(c) Look at each individual under the microscope and record the numbers that have pollen on them.
(d) Draw a pie chart of the results (Exercise 9).

Questions

(1) Which order of insect is most abundant? Suggest reasons for its abundance on the hogweed.
(2) Discuss the other orders collected and suggest reasons for their presence.
(3) Did any animals have pollen on them? If so what does this suggest about these animals, and what might their importance be in the grassland ecosystem?
(4) How meaningful are the answers to question 3 in view of the method used to catch them?
(5) What feature of hogweed might attract insects? Design some laboratory experiments to test your ideas.
(6) What similar experiments could be carried out using flower heads?

Exercise 13: animals of soil and litter

Background

Exercises 9–12 have been concerned with animals above the ground. The litter and soil of grasslands provide a new set of environmental conditions (see section on edaphic factors, p. 79) and microhabitats for a range of different organisms. Species may be macroscopic, i.e. >0.1 mm, for example slugs and insect larvae, or microscopic, for example protozoans. They may live in burrows in the soil, for example earthworms (see Exercise 18), or in the water film around the soil particles, for example nematodes.

The variety and number can be enormous and the activities of these organisms are of great importance in breaking down organic matter (see section on decomposition, p. 60) which in turn affects the soil structure and fertility, and ultimately the vegetation growing in it.

To study the range of organisms living in the litter and soil, different techniques are necessary from those so far described. First, for comparative samples, cores of uniform size need to be taken. A useful tool for this is a hand-held soil sampler that can take surface cores to a depth of 80 cm. These are obtainable from Philip Harris biological suppliers. Alternatively, pieces of plastic drainpipe of known volume can be used. Second, the organisms within the core need to be extracted from the soil and litter; the following techniques may be used:

Flotation technique   When soil is mixed with water, some species will float to the surface. The addition of a salt, for example sodium chloride or magnesium sulphate, will increase the specific gravity of the solution and may cause more species to float to the surface.

Tullgren funnels   This apparatus (Fig. 24) extracts organisms from litter

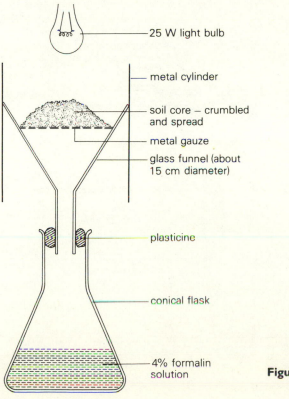

25 W light bulb

metal cylinder

soil core – crumbled and spread

metal gauze

glass funnel (about 15 cm diameter)

plasticine

conical flask

4% formalin solution

Figure 24   Diagram of a Tullgren funnel.

and soil using heat and light. Many organisms show a negative response to these factors and will tend to move away from the source of heat. Such a response will cause them to fall through the gauze into the collecting jar below. Soil samples are placed in the funnel and left for 4 to 5 days, or until the soil is completely dry. Tullgren funnels can be constructed easily and cheaply.

Baermann funnels   This apparatus is used to extract organisms living in the water film around soil particles and is used mainly to extract nematodes which are small, thin, white unsegmented worms. These funnels can also be constructed easily and cheaply (see Fig. 25).

   N.B.   None of these techniques is totally efficient in extracting organisms from the soil and litter, and this should be taken into account when analysing the results obtained from this exercise.

Aim

To extract and compare the range and numbers of organisms found in litter, and the top few centimetres of soil, from two contrasting grasslands using the three techniques described above.

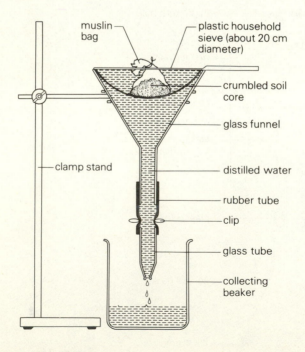

Figure 25   Diagram of a Baermann funnel.

Materials

Surface soil sampler; 30 plastic bags; white trays; water; salt (sodium chloride) (enough to produce a concentrated solution of 400 g per litre); forceps; Petri dishes; 10 Tullgren funnels; 10 Baermann funnels; Key to some common soil organisms (p. 52); microscope.

Time

30 min to take the soil cores; 30 min per core for flotation technique; at least four days for the Tullgren funnel extraction; at least 24 h for the Baermann funnel extraction.

Method

(a) Select two contrasting grasslands, e.g. lawn and uncut verge.
(b) Take 15 soil cores of known volume and depth from the topsoil (plus litter) of each grassland.
(c) Place each core carefully in a plastic bag. Use 5 cores from each area for each of the following techniques:

(i) Flotation: in the laboratory, crumble each core into a white tray; add water or a salt solution. Mix well and allow to settle. Remove the animals that float to the surface; identify them using the key (p. 52) and count the number of individuals of each type that are found.

(ii) Tullgren funnels: crumble one core into each Tullgren funnel and leave with the light on for at least four days, until the soil appears to be completely dry. Extract organisms from the collecting flask. Identify the organisms from each site and record their numbers.

(iii) Baermann funnels: crumble each core into a muslin bag and tie up the top; then place each bag into a Baermann funnel and leave for 24 h. After this time, release the water from the bottom of the funnel by opening the tap. Identify the organisms found and record their numbers. If there are more than can be counted, take 3 to 5 samples of known volume and work out an average number per unit volume. Then multiply up for the total estimated volume collected.

Questions

(1) Compare the numbers and types of organisms extracted overall for each grassland.
(2) Find out what adaptations aid the survival of these organisms in the soil. (Useful books for this include Mc.E. Kevan 1962, and Jackson &

Raw 1966 – see Bibliography.) Use your findings to compare the different sites.

(3) How might the soils of each site have affected the answers to questions 1 and 2?

(4) How could an analysis of aspects of the soil be carried out? (see Exercises 21 to 26).

(5) Discuss the types of organisms extracted by the various techniques and comment on the value of each. Discuss any possible sources of error in the method.

Key 2: to some common soil organisms

1	Locomotory limbs	**2**
	No locomotory limbs.	**19**
2	More than seven pairs of legs.	**3**
	Seven or fewer pairs of legs.	**4**
3	Body segment with typically one pair of legs.	centipede
	Body segment with typically two pairs of legs.	millipede
4	Seven pairs of legs.	woodlouse
	Fewer than seven pairs of legs.	**5**
5	Four pairs of legs.	**6**
	Three pairs of legs.	**8**
6	Resembling a small scorpion with 'lobster-like' claws.	false scorpion
	Not as above.	**7**
7	Body apparently in two parts.	spider
	Body not in two parts and not segmented.	mites
	Body not in two parts but segmented. Two eyes, second pair of legs longer.	harvestman
8	Wings or wing cases.	**9**
	No wings or wing cases.	**16**
9	One pair of wings.	fly (Diptera)
	Two pairs of wings (count wing cases as a pair).	**10**
10	Wings fringed with hairs.	thrips (Thysanoptera)
	Wings not fringed with hairs.	**11**
11	Piercing mouth parts in the form of a beak. Order Hemiptera { heteropteran bug / homopteran bug	
	Mouth parts not as above.	**12**
12	Front wings hard.	**13**
	Front wings membranous.	**15**
13	Appendages at the end of the abdomen modified into stout pincers.	earwig (Dermaptera)
	Not as above.	Order Coleoptera **14**

14	Short wing cases leaving most of the abdomen exposed.	rove beetle
	Head extended into a beak.	weevil
	Antennae with clubs formed by plates.	dung beetle
	Clubbed antennae, 6–9 joints.	palpicorn beetle
	Well developed mandibles, long antennae.	ground beetle
	Tarsi apparently four-jointed.	phytophagous beetle
	Legs and antennae fit closely under body in grooves.	click beetle
	Clubbed antennae.	clavicorn beetle
15	'Waist' between the thorax and abdomen with a node.	ant (Hymenoptera)
	'Waist' between the thorax and abdomen without a node.	ichneumon of chalcid wasp (Hymenoptera)
16	Animal with a 'waist' between thorax and abdomen.	ant
	Not as above.	**17**
17	Animal with a forked springing organ at the hind end.	springtail (Collembola)
	Animal without a forked springing organ at the hind end. Obvious external segmentation.	insect larvae **18**

18	Insect larvae	
	Abdominal stumpy legs (prolegs).	caterpillar (Lepidoptera)
	Last abdominal segment with a pair of forceps.	earwig nymph (Dermaptera)
	Grub-like. Body curved and creamy-white in colour.	Dung beetle larva (Coleoptera)
	Cylindrical body.	wire worm
	Body distinctly flattened, legs short.	silphid beetle larva (Coleoptera)
	Legs six-jointed. Two movable claws.	ground beetle larva (Coleoptera)
	Legs five-jointed. One claw fused with tarsus.	rove beetle larva (Coleoptera)

19	No obvious external segmentation. Shell may be present.	**20**
	Body segmented. No shell.	**23**
20	Very small, no tentacles.	**21**
	Larger, tentacles present.	**22**
21	Body round.	nematode worm
	Body flat.	flatworm
22	External shell present.	snail
	No obvious shell.	slug
23	Body with more than 20 segments.	**24**
	Body with fewer than 20 segments.	**25**

24 White or pink. 'Bristles' (chaetae) usually in
bundles of four.   potworm
Usually brownish. 'Bristles' in pairs.   earthworm
25 Stout, fleshy, usually U-shaped and strongly
curved.   weevil larva (Coleoptera)
Animal without these characteristics.   fly larva (Diptera)

Exercise 14: an estimation of population size for the frog-hopper *Philaenus spumarius*

Background

Philaenus spumarius is a bug of the Order Hemiptera that is abundant in
grasslands (see Fig. 26). It is known as a frog-hopper, spittle bug or cuckoo-
spit insect, and the familiar 'spittle' or froth found on plants is produced by
an aerated sugary secretion from the anus of the nymphs. They hatch in the
spring, from eggs laid in the autumn by females amongst dead plant stems.
The nymphs then climb up the stems, find a site to settle, and suck the plant
sap through piercing mouth parts. The froth is thought to protect the nymphs
from predators and the drying effects of the sun. The adults appear in June
and survive until about late October or early November.

An estimate of the number of adult frog-hoppers in an area of grassland
can be made by a mark–recapture method. This is based on the idea that if a
sample of individuals is marked and returned to the population, when those
individuals have diffused randomly throughout the population then in a
second sample the ratio of marked to unmarked individuals would be in the
same ratio as that of the original number marked to the whole population.
For example, suppose that the total population number (P) of a species is
100. 10 are caught (a), marked and returned to the rest of the population. If
a second sample of 10 is then caught (b), it would be expected that on
average one would be marked (r), i.e.

$$\frac{P}{a} = \frac{b}{r} \text{ or } \frac{100}{10} = \frac{10}{1}$$

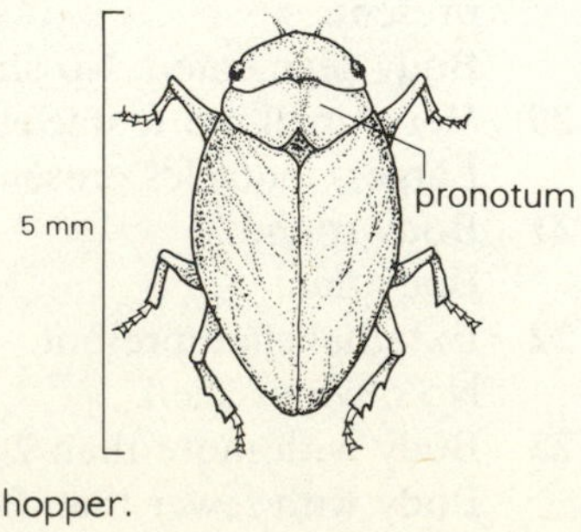

Figure 26 Diagram of *Philaenus spumarius*, the frog-hopper.

So, a population estimate, $\hat{P}$ (where the 'hat' signifies that the number is an estimate and not an absolute value), can be found by applying the formula $\hat{P} = ba/r$, which is called a simple Lincoln Index.

Aim

To estimate the population size of *Philaenus spumarius*, a frog-hopper, in grassland by marking, releasing and recapturing individuals.

Materials

Sweep net; waterproof, fine-tipped, red felt pen; pooter and a few spare collecting tubes with corks; ethyl acetate; cotton wool; about 10 Petri dishes with lids.

Time

1 h to catch, mark and release insects. Warm weather: about 4 h to allow the animals to scatter when released. Cool weather: 24 h to allow the animals to scatter when released. 10 min to recapture.

Time of day

After the dew has dried, or before it has formed.

Time of year

This exercise can be carried out only when the adult frog-hoppers are abundant, i.e. between June and September.

Method

(a) Select an area of rough grassland, bordered if possible, such as by hedges, walls or buildings.
(b) Sweep the area to collect at least 200 frog-hoppers. Transfer them from the sweep net to the collecting tubes using the pooter.
(c) Mark the individuals by making a small spot with the felt-tipped pen on the fore-wings or on the pronotum (the hard plate behind the head: see Fig. 26)
(d) After they are marked, place the frog-hoppers in Petri dishes to recover. Allow them plenty of space (about 20 individuals to a dish) and cover with a lid.

> N.B. If the insects are too active to mark, wedge a small piece of cotton wool dipped in ethyl acetate in the top of the collecting tube, using the cork to hold the cotton wool in place (this way the cotton wool can be easily removed). Great care and observation are needed here – too much ethyl acetate will kill the frog-hoppers. When some begin to stagger a little and some are still hopping, quickly remove the cotton wool. In a few seconds most will be ready for marking.

(e)   After recovery, record the number marked, discounting and removing any dead or damaged individuals.

(f)   Scatter the frog-hoppers throughout the area studied.

(g)   Return about 4 h later if in warm weather, or 24 h later if cool, and sweep the grassland again until at least the number first netted (a) have been caught.

(h)   Slow frog-hopper activity down if necessary and retain all individuals until steps (i) and (j) have been completed.

(i)   Record the total number caught (b).

(j)   Record the total number recaptured, i.e. marked (r).

(k)   Return all individuals to the grassland.

(l)   Calculate the estimated population size using the simple Lincoln Index:

$$\hat{P} = \frac{ab}{r}$$

where $\hat{P}$ = total population estimate
   a = number of frog-hoppers marked in first sample,
   b = number of frog-hoppers captured in second sample,
   r = number of frog-hoppers recaptured, i.e. marked.

Questions

(1)   It is assumed that the population size of frog-hoppers remains constant for the duration of the exercise. What assumptions, therefore, are being made about (a) the effect of marking on individuals, and (b) movement of individuals into (immigration) and out of (emigration) the area studied?

(2)   What other factors might have altered the population size and what assumptions are we making about them?

(3)   How is it assumed that marked individuals have mixed within the population? How could you test to see if this assumption was true?

(4)   Of the other grassland species you have encountered, which do you think might be suitable for population size estimates using the mark–recapture method? Give reasons for your suggestions, and if possible, test your ideas.

Exercise 15: small mammals in grassland

Background

The small mammal most commonly found in grasslands is the field vole, a grey–brown animal with small ears and eyes, blunt snout and short tail.

Voles tend to be found in rough, ungrazed grassland, and evidence of their presence can be seen in runways amongst dense vegetation. They are primarily herbivorous, feeding mainly on grass stems and leaves, and on occasion, when populations become large, can damage areas of grassland. They provide an important element in the diet of owls and birds of prey, as well as larger mammals such as stoats and weasels. After myxomatosis had caused the decline of rabbits, voles also became a very important food source for foxes.

Other small mammals that might be observed in grassland include the woodmouse and shrew. The mainly herbivorous woodmouse is more typically found in woodlands, but shrews are often found in grass and are insectivorous, feeding mainly on earthworms, spiders and woodlice. Below the surface of some grasslands, for example permanent pastures, the insectivorous mole can be found living in tunnels.

Small mammals such as voles and woodmice can be caught and studied using a small aluminium trap, the Longworth trap (see Fig. 27a, b). This consists of two parts: the tunnel and the nest box. The tunnel is fitted with a trap door, which is closed by a bar at the opposite end from the door. The nest box is attached to the tunnel, and is loosely packed with hay, for bedding, as well as some food, such as cereal, nuts, apple or carrot, to prevent death from cold and starvation.

The trap is set with the nest box at a slight downward angle, so that urine and moisture will drain away. The trap can be set to remain open, and baited, to allow animals to become familiar with it before any study is begun.

Notes on small mammal trapping and handling

(a) Look for small pathways, tunnels or runways, made by mammals amongst the vegetation, when setting traps. Place the traps along the runs or at the entrance to tunnels, trying to create as little disturbance as possible (Fig. 27b).

(b) Always mark trap sites to minimise the risk of mammals dying in a lost trap.

(c) *Never* handle mammals directly. If necessary, use strong-fabric gloves, e.g. gardening gloves.

(d) To remove animals from traps, place whole trap upside-down in a plastic bag, holding nest box at the top of the bag. Check that the animal is not in the tunnel, and carefully remove it. Ease the animal into the bag and then transfer it into a container, with a lid, for observation.

(e) Provide food and straw.

(f) Should shrews be caught, they will not survive long without food, and should be provided with worms or instantly released. (Essential reading: Gurnell & Flowerdew 1982 – see Bibliography.)

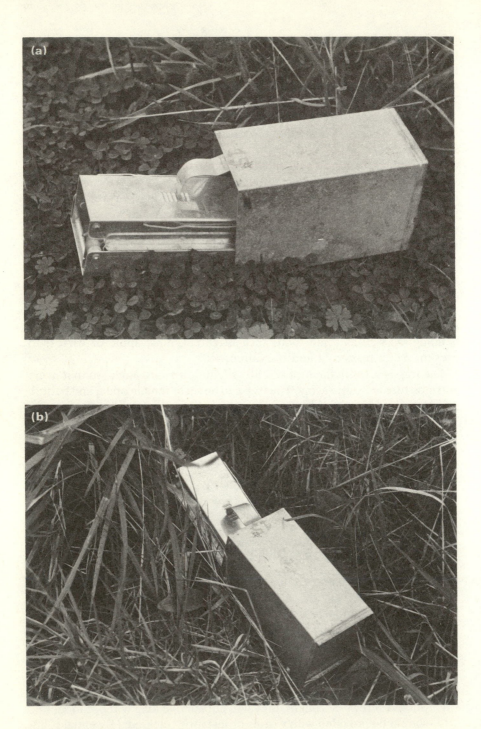

Figure 27   (a) The Longworth trap; (b) the trap set.

Aim

To study the mammals and their activity in a grassland.

Materials

25 Longworth traps; straw and food, e.g. cereal, nuts, apple, carrot; 25 canes; plastic bag; containers, e.g. perspex aquaria.

Time

1 week.

Method

(a) Set 25 Longworth traps in an area of long grass. Suitable sites are areas that back on to scrub.
(b) Fix doors to remain open and leave the traps baited for 24 h.
(c) Unlock doors and leave.
(d) Check traps at 9 a.m. and 9 p.m. daily for a week.
(e) Record numbers and species found at each time.

N.B.   To know which animals have been caught, it is possible to mark them by picking them up by the scruff of the neck and clipping a little bit of fur from the back.

An estimate of the population size of voles can be made by carrying out a mark–recapture experiment. Set a known number of traps. Mark and release any voles that are caught. Reset the traps and note how many voles are caught and the number of marked individuals re-caught, when the traps are next checked. See Exercise 14 for details of how to estimate the population size.

Questions

(1) How many mammals were caught during the course of the exercise and which species was most common?
(2) At what time of day were the mammals most often caught? What does this imply about their activity?
(3) Discuss the numbers in relation to: (i) the time of year; (ii) the type of grassland; (iii) the vegetation or features bordering the grassland.
(4) Some animals having been caught once, may choose to return to the trap, knowing that there will be food and warmth for a while before being released; these are called 'trap-happy' animals. Conversely, some animals will not return once caught and are called 'trap-shy' animals. Discuss the implications of this for the results.

Decomposition analysis

Background

Decomposition is the process whereby organic matter derived from such sources as dead plants and animals, and eliminated waste material (faeces, urine) are changed physically and chemically by a group of organisms called the decomposers. Important organisms are bacteria and fungi, which derive their energy from the organic matter, and at the same time release vital nutrients back into the soil for re-use.

The end products of decomposition include carbon dioxide, ammonia and nitrogen, sulphur and phosphorus compounds as well as complex organic residues that are resistant to further change.

All organisms depend on nutrients for healthy growth. Plants absorb minerals via their roots and incorporate them into their cells. If certain nutrients are lacking, then energy flow (see Exercise 19) can be impeded or stopped altogether. Nutrient deficiencies in plants are revealed by their physical appearances, for example, a plant lacking nitrogen will be yellow, and stunted.

Decomposition can be divided broadly into two main parts:

(a) Decomposition requiring a highly active microflora, which is usually associated with well aerated, neutral or slightly acid soils, such as might occur in cultivated pastures. The bacteria and fungi provide a food source for soil protozoans, which in turn are fed upon by other soil animals, forming an important part in the detritus or decomposer food chain (see Exercise 19).

(b) Physical incorporation of material requiring an active fauna in the soil. Earthworms in particular play an important role in this respect.

Exercises 16 to 18 aim to illustrate:

(a) the sequence of events in the decomposition of organic matter in grasslands, and the effects of different sizes of organisms (Exercises 16 and 17).

(b) the role of earthworms in the physical incorporation of material into the soil.

Exercise 16: the colonisation and decomposition of cellophane in the soil

Background

The colonisation and decomposition of plant material appear to follow a distinct sequence of events, or a succession (see Exercise 8). Fungi usually colonise first, followed by bacteria; these then provide food for nematodes and protozoans. Other animals, for example, mites, may graze on the decomposing cellulose, and everything might be ingested by earthworms. One way to study this colonisation is to use cellophane as a source of cellulose, which is attacked by organisms that normally colonise the cellulose found in plant remains.

Aim

To study the colonisation and decomposition of cellophane over a period of time in a grassland soil.

Materials

Forceps; cellophane squares 1 × 1 cm, 4 squares per week. (The cellophane should be preboiled in distilled water to remove any soluble plasticisers.); 10 glass microscope slides (1 per week); microscope; cotton blue in lactophenol dye; 10 markers, for example, short canes; trowel.

Time

10 weeks.

Method

(a) Space out 4 cellophane squares on each microscope slide, and press in place using forceps.
(b) Bury each slide separately in a small area of grassland by digging a small hole with the trowel, placing the slide in vertically, and then covering with soil.
(c) Make sure that the position of each slide is clearly marked and that the area is not disturbed.
(d) Once a week for 10 weeks, carefully remove a slide from the soil.
(e) Mount the slide in cotton blue in lactophenol to stain any organisms present.
(f) Identify the types of organisms and list and record approximate numbers. Make a sketch of the four cellophane squares on each slide.
(g) Use the results to work out the pattern of colonisation.

N.B.   This study can be continued for longer than 10 weeks by setting up more slides initially.

Questions

(1)   Make a summary of the sequence of events that has occurred, noting when each change takes place.
(2)   Suggest reasons for each event.
(3)   Is there any evidence to suggest that competition between species is taking place?
(4)   What factors might affect the rate of decomposition?

Exercise 17: the colonisation and decomposition of leaf litter in the soil

Background

Exercise 16 shows that different organisms are present at different stages in the decomposition of organic matter, but it does not take into account their size or behaviour. By controlling the size of organisms that can play a part in decomposition, feeding habits can be studied, as well as the way different organisms deal with material. The effect of organism size is investigated by burying pieces of leaves in bags of different mesh size.

Aim

To study the colonisation and decomposition of leaf litter in a grassland soil for different sizes of organisms.

Materials

Leaves of one plant species, e.g. sycamore; scalpel; four nets of mesh about 10 mm, e.g. hair net (A); four nets of mesh about 1 mm, e.g. net curtain (B); four nets of mesh about 0.25 mm, e.g. fine weave synthetic material (C); twelve canes; nylon thread.

Time

At least 6 months.

Method

(a)   Cut out 40 rectangles of leaf, each 10 × 20 mm, and place 10 in each net A.
(b)   Repeat (a) for nets B and C.

(c)   Tie up the nets with a nylon thread to form loose bags.
(d)   Place the 12 bags in the topsoil of the grassland to be studied, marking
      each with a cane.
(e)   At monthly intervals remove the bags from the soil and take them to
      the laboratory.
(f)   Very carefully take out the leaf rectangles and:

    (i)   count the number of rectangles;
    (ii)   measure the area of any section removed (this can be done by
         placing the leaf rectangles on squared paper);
    (iii) mount in water and examine under the microscope;
    (iv)   identify and record the organisms present.

(g)   Return the leaves to the nets and place them back in the soil.
(h)   Repeat (f) at monthly intervals for at least 6 months.

Questions

(1)   Which group of leaves appears to have decreased most in size? Suggest
      reasons why this might be so.
(2)   Does there appear to be a correlation between the way organic matter
      is removed and the types of organisms observed?
(3)   Discuss the decomposition of leaves over time in relation to mesh size.
(4)   What factors other than mesh size might be affecting the results?
(5)   Give reasons why different types of grassland soil may produce differ-
      ent results from those that you have observed.
(6)   Design an experiment to test some of the ideas you have put forward in
      question 5. (See Exercises 22–26.)
(7)   Discuss any problems that have arisen during the course of this
      experiment.

Exercise 18: the role of earthworms in decomposition

Background

Earthworms, commonly found in grasslands, play a very important role in
the decomposition of organic matter by moving the soil while feeding. They
ingest plant debris, especially leaves, together with mineral particles of the
soil, partially digest the organic matter, i.e. plant debris, and undigested
material is released as worm casts either below the ground or at the surface.
This moving of the soil incorporates air and organic matter into the substrate, improving fertility and rendering material into smaller fragments for
attack by bacteria and fungi.

    For earthworms to thrive, they require certain conditions. In general they
are intolerant of frost and drought and are therefore absent in sandy or very

shallow soils. They prefer an aerated habitat and as a consequence are rare in heavy or undrained soils. They have a continuous requirement for calcium and do not thrive in acid soils. If conditions are suitable earthworm numbers, and the amount of earth they move, can be very high indeed.

There are about 25 species of earthworm in Britain, of which about 10 are common in gardens and agricultural land. One of the most common species of earthworm in this country is *Lumbricus terrestris*, which can be found in grasslands, particularly where they are overhung by trees. It lives in a U-shaped burrow which it plugs with leaves, and it produces casts below the surface of the soil. It is a brownish-red worm that can easily be identified by looking at the anterior segments (see Fig. 28).

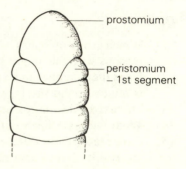

Figure 28   Diagram of the anterior segments
of *Lumbricus terrestris*. Scale: ×16.

Aims

(1)   To investigate the burial of leaf litter by *Lumbricus terrestris* in grass-land.
(2)   To determine the number and biomass of earthworms in relation to the burial of leaf litter.

Time

At least 1 month for (1) and 1 h for (2).

Time of year

Autumn, at leaf fall.

Materials

6 l of water and formalin solution, containing 25 cm³ of 40% formalin per litre; 10 m tape; 6 × 1 m² cages: wooden frames covered by chicken wire (about 2 cm mesh; see Fig. 29); collecting dish; balance; hand lens ×10.

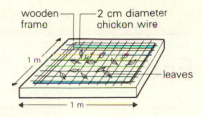

Figure 29 Diagram of the type of cage to be used in Exercise 18.

Method

(a) Select an area of grassland shaded by trees.

(b) Collect 10 batches of 100 leaves.

(c) Dry at 60°C and weigh four batches separately. Use these four values to estimate the dry weights of the remaining six batches of leaves.

(d) Place the 1 m² cages in two rows of three, 3 m apart, removing any leaves from beneath them.

(e) Weigh the remaining six batches of leaves and scatter one batch beneath each cage.

(f) After at least a month, count the number of leaves under each cage. Wash them to remove any soil and dry at 60°C.

(g) When dry (leave at least 2 h), weigh the leaves.

(h) To determine the number and biomass of earthworms, pour 1 l of water and formalin solution into each cage area. Wait for about 5 min until the worms begin to appear on the surface.

(i) Record the numbers of *L. terrestris* that emerge until all activity ceases.

(j) Weigh the worms from each cage.

(k) As quickly as possible after the worms have emerged, rinse then in fresh water and return them to the grassland.

(l) For each cage, plot the number and weight of leaves buried against the weight of *L. terrestris*.

Questions

(1) Is there a correlation between the number or biomass of *L. terrestris* and the decrease in the weight of leaves over time?

(2) What effects, other than that of the worms, might be causing a decrease in the weight of leaves on the surface?

(3) What factors might influence the rate of activity of the earthworms in removing the leaves?

(4) Design an experiment to test the effects of temperature on earthworm activity.

(5) Design an experiment to test the hypothesis that *L. terrestris* has a preference for leaves of a certain species.

(6) Calculate an average number and average biomass of *L. terrestris* in 1 m² of grassland.

(7) What features of the soil could be tested in the area where this study was carried out? (See Exercises 23–26.)

Energy flow

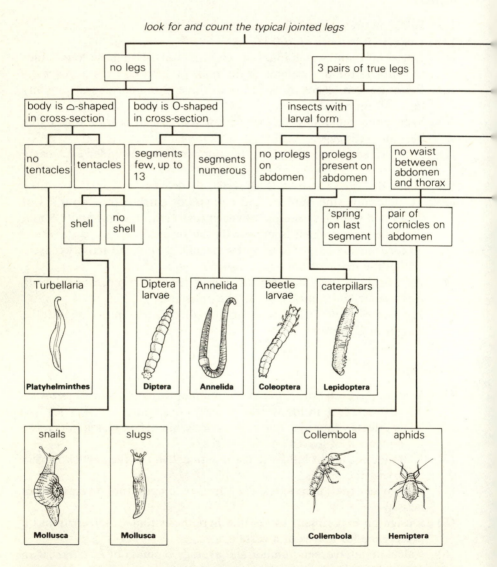

Figure 30 A key to invertebrate animals found in turf. (From Jenkins, P. F. 1976. *School grounds: some ecological enquiries*. London: Heinemann; reprinted by permission.)

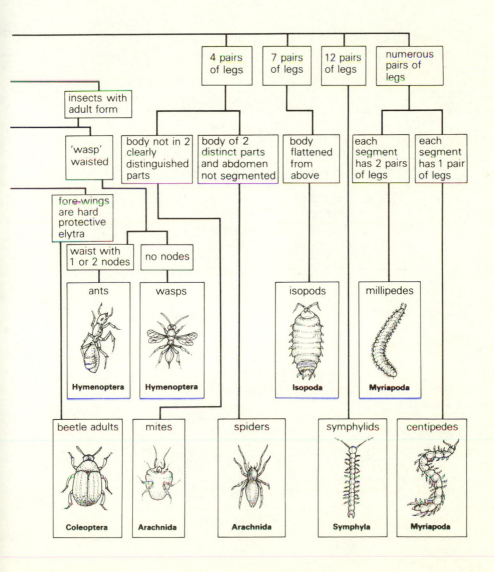

4 pairs of legs

7 pairs of legs

12 pairs of legs

numerous pairs of legs

insects with adult form

'wasp' waisted

body not in 2 clearly distinguished parts

body of 2 distinct parts and abdomen not segmented

body flattened from above

each segment has 2 pairs of legs

each segment has 1 pair of legs

fore-wings are hard protective elytra

waist with 1 or 2 nodes

no nodes

ants

Hymenoptera

wasps

Hymenoptera

isopods

Isopoda

millipedes

Myriapoda

beetle adults

Coleoptera

mites

Arachnida

spiders

Arachnida

symphylids

Symphyla

centipedes

Myriapoda

Table 4 Diets of animals found in soil and turf: H = herbivore; D = detritivore; C = carnivore; O = omnivore.

Group		Diet	Type of feeding
Platyhelminthes			
turbellarians	flatworms	microscopic animals of water film	C
Annelida			
oligochaetes	earthworms	bacteria, fungi, plant detritus	H D
	potworms	fungi and nematodes	H
Insecta			
Collembola	springtails	bacteria, fungi, plant detritus	H D
Orthoptera	crickets and grasshoppers	mainly plant roots, tubers, grass	H
Coleoptera	beetles:		
	(i) ground and rove beetles	predatory	C
	(ii) weevils	plant material	H
	(iii) dor beetles	scavenging	O
	(iv) ladybirds	attack scale insects, aphids and larvae of many insects	C
Diptera	flies		
	(i) larvae	dung, animal detritus, carrion, fungus	H or C
	(ii) adults	dung, animal detritus, carrion	H C D
	(iii) leather jackets	plant material	H
Hymenoptera	ants	predatory on immature macrofauna	C
Hemiptera	bugs and aphids	plant sucking	H
Dermaptera	earwigs	flower petals, carrion, other insects	O
Lepidoptera	moths and butterflies:		
	(i) caterpillars	plant material	H
	(ii) pupae	non-feeding	
Arachnida	mites	bacteria, fungi and detritus	mainly D
	spiders	insects and other small animals	C

Table 4 continued

Myriapoda	centipedes	insects and other small-scale animals	C
	millipedes	wood, plant detritus	H D
Crustacea	woodlice	dead plant or animal matter	D
Mollusca	snails	plant material	H

Exercise 19: energy flow within the grassland ecosystem

Background

The primary producers of the grassland ecosystem, manufacturing complex organic compounds from simple inorganic ones using the sun's energy, are green plants. Dependent on them for essential food are the consumers. These comprise herbivores grazing directly on the vegetation, for example, slugs, snails, voles, sheep, rabbits, and carnivores feeding indirectly by preying on the herbivores or other carnivores, for example, spiders and centipedes. The transfer of energy through the organisms is referred to as a food chain and positions along it are called trophic levels.

It is convenient to recognise two food chains:

(a) Grazing food chain, i.e. plant → herbivore → carnivore.
(b) Detritus or decomposer food chain. Ultimately all organisms die; this dead organic matter (detritus) forms the basis of the detritus or decomposer food chain (see decomposition analysis p. 60). Detritivores, for example, earthworms and woodlice, feed on detritus, and are, in their turn, preyed upon.

At each trophic level energy is lost owing to respiration, activity and incomplete digestion. Consequently there is less energy available for each level, so numbers generally decrease. Size, on the other hand, tends to increase. These relationships can be represented by a pyramid of numbers or pyramid of biomass (biomass is the mass of living material at any one time).

Aims

(1) To determine numbers and biomass relationships in grassland for the vegetation and top 10 cm of soil.
(2) To construct a food web.

Materials

Knife; 10 plastic bags; two 30-m tapes; 10 sets of 4-figure random numbers from 00 to 30; Petri dishes; balance; Key to invertebrate animals found in turf (Fig. 30); Diets of animals found in soil and turf (Table 4).

Time

3½ h.

Method 1

(a) Locate ten sampling sites, using random numbers, in the grassland to be studied (see Exercise 4).
(b) At each site, remove a cube of vegetation 10 × 10 × 10 cm.
(c) Place each sample in a plastic bag.
(d) In the laboratory, carefully hand-sort the sample into plant and animal material. Roots can be extracted at the end by washing off remaining soil.
(e) Identify the animals using Figure 30.
(f) Sort the animals into herbivores, detritivores and carnivores, using the information given in Table 4.
(g) Count the numbers of herbivores, detritivores and carnivores. If there is more than one food source, for example herbivore and detritivore, split the numbers in half. Count omnivores as carnivores.
(h) Weigh the vegetation, herbivores, detritivores and carnivores.
(i) Convert the numbers and biomass to percentages and record in table form as illustrated below:

	NUMBERS		BIOMASS	
FEEDING LEVEL	Number	Percentages	Fresh wt (g)	Percentages
CARNIVORES				
HERBIVORES				
DETRITIVORES				
VEGETATION	/////	/////		

Method 2

Construct a food web for the organisms you have obtained. See Fig. 31 for the format.

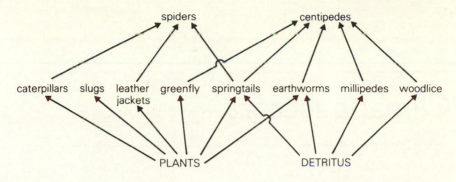

Figure 31 A simplified food web for grassland turf and soil. The arrows represent the direction of flow of energy.

Questions

(1) Discuss the relationship between the numbers of organisms.
(2) Does the biomass decrease in the same proportions as the numbers? If not, suggest reasons for this.
(3) Water makes up a large proportion of organisms, but is of little importance in terms of energetics. Why do you think wet weight was used?
(4) Discuss some of the problems that have arisen in compiling the numbers and biomass relationships at all stages of the investigation. Attempt to put forward ways of solving them.
(5) What does the food web tell us about feeding relationships in the soil?

Climatic factors

Exercise 20: the recording of climatic factors

Background

The distribution and abundance of species are affected by climatic factors which include temperature, precipitation in various forms, humidity, wind and light. Open grassland, unlike woodland, for example, where the trees ameliorate climatic conditions, is greatly influenced by variation in the weather. However, a microclimate prevails amongst the vegetation and this varies depending on the height of the vegetation and the degree of exposure of the grassland site.

In tall grass, as one descends through the vegetation:

light decreases,
humidity increases,
wind speed decreases, and
temperatures may increase, then decrease near the soil.

In short grass these effects are far less marked.

Temperature   This is the major factor limiting the distribution of plants and animals in the world. It varies with latitude, altitude, daily and seasonally. Temperature may directly influence survival, reproduction and development of organisms. Indirect effects may limit distributions by affecting competitive ability, disease resistance, predation and parasitism.

Air temperature can be measured in the shade using a thermometer.

Precipitation   The quantity and pattern of precipitation determines the main vegetational areas of the world. It may follow a seasonal cycle as well as showing short-term fluctuations. Precipitation can be divided into two parts:

(a)   actual rainfall, which is precipitation from clouds;
(b)   effective rainfall, which is the water available after such things as evaporation, interception and runoff have been taken into account.

Figure 32 A standard five-inch rain gauge.

Rainfall can be measured using a rain gauge (see Fig. 32); this consists of a five-inch diameter funnel plus collecting bottle which may be buried in the ground. The volume of water in the collecting bottle is measured daily by tipping the contents into a measuring cylinder.

Humidity The level of atmospheric humidity directly affects transpiration and is therefore one of the major factors that determines the habitat of a plant. It can be measured using a whirling hygrometer (see Fig. 33); this consists of wet and dry bulb thermometers mounted in a frame, with a handle that allows the frame to be rotated. The hygrometer is whirled in the air until the two thermometers give constant readings. The relative humidity can then be calculated using either a slide rule supplied with the whirling hygrometer, or by using hygrometric tables.

Wind Wind has several important effects; it increases evaporation and therefore transpiration; causes mechanical damage; creates waves; circulates oxygen, carbon dioxide and water vapour; aids dispersal of seeds and

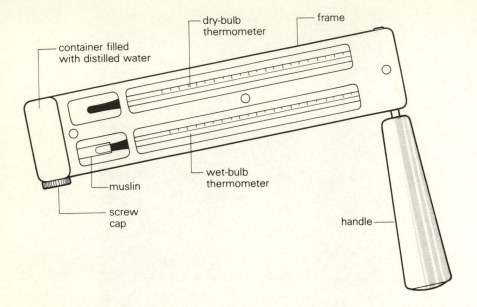

Figure 33 Diagram of a whirling hygrometer used for measuring relative humidity.

fruits; and gives rise to wind pruning. Wind pruning takes place when buds on the windward side of trees and shrubs are killed by drying and freezing, which are accelerated by the wind; near the sea, salt spray aids this process.

Wind may also determine the type of vegetation; this is seen on sea cliffs having a cliff progression: from grassland through to bracken, scrub and finally trees in sheltered areas.

Wind speed can be measured using a hand-held windmeter (see Fig. 34); it is held facing the wind, and a direct indication of the speed is given by a small sphere moving in a vertical tube.

Light   Light provides the energy needed by green plants for photosynthesis. It may also be a stimulus for plant and animal reproduction.

The measurement of climatic factors will provide additional information for any site being investigated, especially if comparative results are taken, as outlined in this exercise. For long-term investigations of climatic changes, a weather station can be set up with a variety of recording instruments (see Fig. 35 a–d).

Aim

To study variations in ground temperature, air temperature, relative humidity, wind speed and light, for two areas within a grassland.

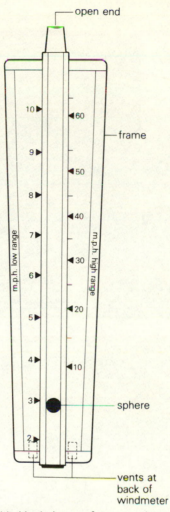

open end

10 ▶
◀ 60
frame
9 ▶
◀ 50
8 ▶
◀ 40
m.p.h. low range
7 ▶
m.p.h. high range
◀ 30
6 ▶
◀ 20
5 ▶
4 ▶
◀ 10
3 ▶
sphere
2 ▶
vents at
back of
windmeter

Figure 34   Diagram of a hand-held windmeter for measuring wind speed.

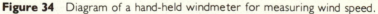

Materials

Thermometer; whirling hygrometer; hand-held windmeter; light meter.

Time

15 min.

Method

(a)   Select a grassland site.

(b)   In the centre of the site carry out the following steps:

Figure 35 (a) An example of a Stevenson screen used for housing thermometers to measure air temperature. (b) A view inside the Stevenson screen. (c) This shows a grass minimum thermometer (left) which records the temperature of the ground. A soil thermometer is buried to a depth of 30 cm at right. (d) This is an example of a sunshine recorder. The glass sphere concentrates the sun's rays onto a card which is marked in hours.

Figure 35 continued

(i) Place the thermometer on the ground, allow to stabilise, and record the temperature.

(ii) Record relative humidity by whirling the hygrometer until the temperature readings are constant – about 2 min. Record wet and dry bulb temperatures; the latter will automatically give a reading of air temperature. Calculate the relative humidity.

(iii) Record the wind speed using the hand-held windmeter.

(c) Repeat the whole procedure at the edge of the field.

Questions

(1) Comment on the results for both sites.

(2) What is bordering the area studied? Could this be influencing the results in any way?

(3) What effect might each factor studied be having on the plants and animals of both sites?

(4) Criticise the techniques.

(5) Design a study to compare changes in microclimate over time for a grassland and another suitable habitat, e.g. a woodland or a hedge.

Edaphic factors

Background

Edaphic factors are those that affect plant and animal life through the soil.

Soil can be defined as the superficial covering of the earth's crust and the material in which plant roots obtain water and essential nutrients. It is therefore one of the most important materials on earth. It is mainly formed by a combination of two processes:

(a) the breakdown of rock by erosion – inorganic material;
(b) the formation of humus from dead organisms – organic material.

Both processes are affected by living organisms, for example fungi, bacteria and earthworms.

The type of soil depends on the underlying bedrock. Acid rocks, for example sandstones, break down to form acid soils. Alkaline rocks, for example chalk and limestone, break down to form alkaline soils.

Particle size plays a large part in determining the characteristics of a soil. For example, it affects drainage and temperature. A soil with large particles such as sand, will have good drainage, will therefore be well aerated and will warm up quickly in the spring. A soil with small particles such as clay will have poor drainage, remaining waterlogged for a longer period, and be slow to warm up. This is because water has a higher specific heat than air.

The soil, therefore plays a large part in determining the vegetation present. In grassland ecosystems, for example, heavy soils with a highly soluble alkaline content support such species as the common meadow grasses (*Poa spp.*), crested dog's tail (*Cynosurus cristatus*), perennial rye grass (*Lolium perenne*) and cock's foot (*Dactylis glomerata*), whereas on siliceous (acid) rock in many northern and western areas, the grassland is dominated by common bent (*Agrostis tenuis*) and sheep's fescue (*Festuca ovina*).

Not only does the soil determine the species present, but conversely the vegetation has a marked influence upon the soil. In sandy soils, grasses will help to bind the soil together, improving moisture retention and preventing erosion. In clay soils the roots will effectively increase the soil permeability, thereby improving drainage and aeration.

This section (Exercises 21–26) aims to highlight some of the main characteristics of the soil.

N.B. To understand the ecological significance of edaphic factors, the exercises in this section should be carried out as comparisons between different grassland soils, rather than as isolated examples (see Introduction).

An account of the accompanying vegetation is also useful, and it is suggested that the exercises be carried out in conjunction with Exercise 4. Soil for Exercises 23 to 26 can be collected from random quadrats after you have recorded the plant species.

Exercise 21: the soil profile

Background

Soil is often stratified into distinct layers known as horizons which differ in physical, chemical and biological characteristics. In a normal mineral soil there are three main horizons:

> A   horizon: topsoil
> B   horizon: subsoil
> C   horizon: parent material

The internal arrangement of these layers is known as the soil profile and forms the basis of soil classification. A profile will provide useful information about the rooting systems of plants as well as other soil features.

Aim

To investigate the soil profile of a grassland.

Materials

Spade; metre rule.

Time

45 min in the field; a further 2 h at least if moisture content and organic matter are determined.

Method

(a)   Choose a relatively undisturbed area of the site to be studied.
(b)   Dig a small pit down to the subsoil, leaving a clean vertical face.
(c)   Make a sketch of the profile.
(d)   Measure the depth of the different layers.

(e) Record the colour by smearing a little soil on to the recording sheet.

(f) Make notes about the following:

  (i) texture – use the scheme for finger assessment of soil texture (see Exercise 26);

  (ii) water content – to measure this, see Exercise 24;

  (iii) proportion and nature of stones present;

  (iv) distribution and type of organic matter – see Exercise 25 to measure this;

  (v) presence and nature of root material.

(g) Use the format of Fig. 36 as a guide to recording the soil profile.

If it is impossible to dig a pit, a soil auger can be used to obtain a profile. The auger is screwed into the ground to a depth of 15 cm and pulled straight out. Describe the soil obtained from the auger as outlined above. The soil is then removed from the auger which is returned to the original hole. Further samples are taken until the auger will go no deeper. Soil can be collected from the auger thread for each 15-cm sample, if wanted for further analysis.

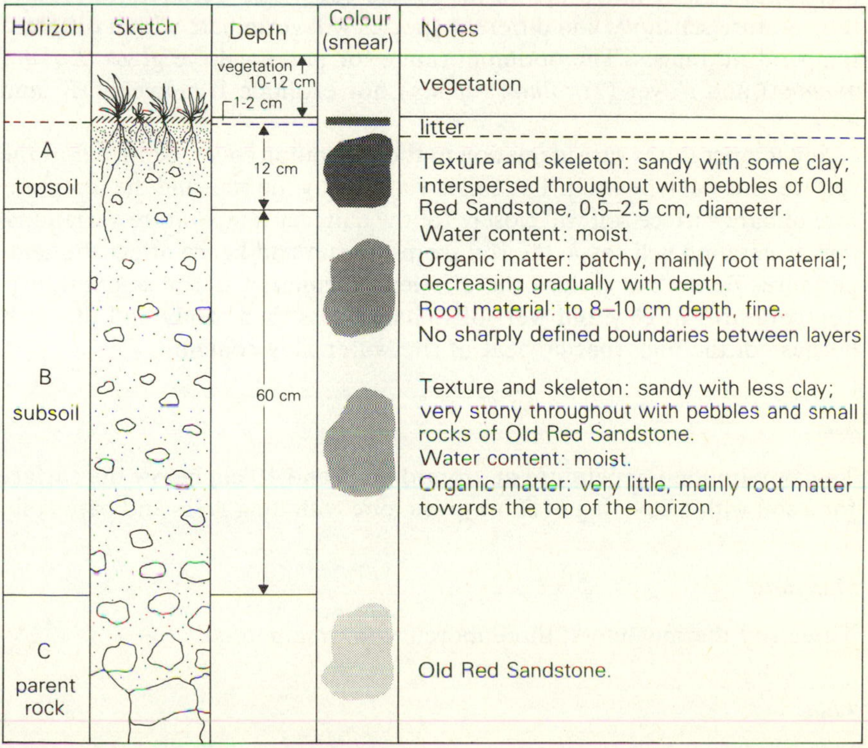

Horizon	Sketch	Depth	Colour (smear)	Notes
		vegetation 10–12 cm 1–2 cm		vegetation
				litter
A topsoil		12 cm		Texture and skeleton: sandy with some clay; interspersed throughout with pebbles of Old Red Sandstone, 0.5–2.5 cm, diameter. Water content: moist. Organic matter: patchy, mainly root material; decreasing gradually with depth. Root material: to 8–10 cm depth, fine. No sharply defined boundaries between layers
B subsoil		60 cm		Texture and skeleton: sandy with less clay; very stony throughout with pebbles and small rocks of Old Red Sandstone. Water content: moist. Organic matter: very little, mainly root matter towards the top of the horizon.
C parent rock				Old Red Sandstone.

Figure 36 An example of a soil profile.

Questions

(1) Summarise your observations of the soil.
(2) Is there a lot of undecomposed material present?
(3) What does your answer to question 2 suggest about the fertility of the soil?
(4) How does the vegetation appear to be affecting the nature of the soil?

Exercise 22: the recording of soil temperature

Background

The temperature of the soil plays a very important role in determining the metabolic rates of the vegetation and organisms associated with it. There is a decrease in metabolic activity as enzyme reactions are slowed down, therefore in cold weather the rate of absorption by roots and underground storage organs is reduced, so that less water is available to the plants. The decay of organic matter virtually ceases in the winter because of the reduced metabolic rate of micro-organisms in the soil. Seed germination is also temperature sensitive, and different species will germinate within different temperature ranges. The optimum range for perennial rye grass (*Lolium perenne*) and clover (*Trifolium repens*), for example is between 18° and 23°C.

Soil temperatures vary in relation to the vegetation cover, depth below the surface and soil type itself. The soil is warmed by the sun, and the temperature of bare surface soil will closely follow daily air temperature variations. Any vegetation will shade the soil from the sun and hence affect the temperature. Below the surface there is less fluctuation in soil temperature. Temperatures of clay and wet soils change less than sandy and dry soils because of the high specific heat of the water they contain.

Aim

To compare the temperature at ground level and 10 cm below the surface for a soil with a covering of short grass, one with long grass and bare soil.

Materials

Three soil thermometers; three mercury thermometers.

Time

2–3 weeks for the grass to grow; 15 min to clear an area of vegetation; 10 min to set up the thermometers; 24 h to monitor temperatures.

Method

(a) In a lawn or playing field, set up three plots at one metre intervals, as described below:
  (i) long grass: leave an area of about 1 m² uncut for 2–3 weeks depending on the time of year;
  (ii) short grass: mown grass;
  (iii) bare soil: clear an area of about 20 × 20 cm of vegetation, removing as much root material as possible, a day before the insertion of a thermometer. This will allow the temperature of the soil to adjust for the absence of vegetation.

(b) Place a mercury thermometer on the ground in each plot.

(c) Insert a soil thermometer 10 cm into the soil about 5 cm away from each mercury thermometer.

(d) Allow the thermometers to equilibrate with the surroundings and then record the temperature.

(e) Continue to take readings at hourly intervals for 24 h, always reading the thermometers in the same sequence.

(f) Plot a graph of time against temperature for each set of results.

Recording the soil temperature over a period of time would make an interesting project. For example, readings from the soil surface, and at a constant depth, once a day could be taken over a month. The graph in Fig. 37 shows the temperatures taken once a day in short grass at a depth of

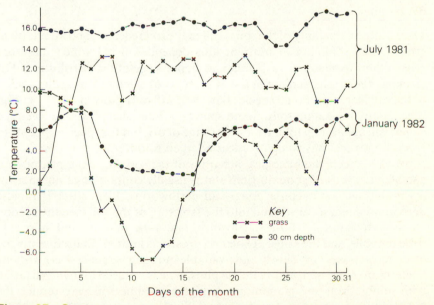

Figure 37 Graph to show the results of temperature recordings taken at the ground surface and at a depth of 30 m below short grass for two contrasting months.

30 cm for two contrasting months. The temperature of the soil in the cleared plot (see (iii), bare soil, described above) could be monitored as the vegetation recolonises. Soil temperatures in different grasslands could also be studied.

Questions

(1) What effect does the vegetation appear to be having on the soil temperature at and below the surface for each of the three plots?
(2) Discuss the implications of your findings for the micro-organisms in the soil for the three plots studied (see Exercises 16–18).
(3) How might grazing affect the temperature of the soil in contrast to mowing?
(4) What other biotic (living) and abiotic (non-living) factors will be influencing the results obtained, apart from the depth of the soil and the vegetation?

Exercise 23: the determination of soil pH

Background

The acidity or alkalinity of the soil is called the soil reaction, and affects plant growth. The solubility of nutrient ions depends on pH which therefore affects their availability to plants and hence vegetation distribution. For example, there is a decrease in the availability of calcium ions as the acidity of the soil increases. Some species however, will only grow in acid soils, and others only in alkaline soils. Some species such as sheep's fescue (*Festuca ovina*) will apparently tolerate a wide range of pH, but the species appears to comprise several physiological races adapted to different pH levels.

pH also affects the biological activities of the soil. For example, neutral and alkaline soils of good nutrient status usually contain large numbers of organisms such as bacteria, fungi and earthworms. Plant litter is rapidly decomposed and incorporated into the structure of the soil (see the section on decomposition, p. 60). Earthworms are rare in acid and nutrient-deficient soils, and the range of bacteria present is limited. Consequently the litter decomposes very slowly and available nitrogen is reduced as nitrifying bacteria are repressed, and available phosphate is reduced following fixation with soluble iron and aluminium. A highly alkaline soil may reduce the availability of certain nutrients, especially the trace elements (i.e. those required in minute quantities) manganese and boron.

Soil pH ranges can roughly be divided into five parts:

pH 4.0–5.5   strongly acid
pH 5.5–6.5   moderately acid
pH 6.5–7.5   neutral
pH 7.5–8.5   moderately alkaline
pH 8.5–10.0 strongly alkaline.

There are various ways of measuring soil reaction or pH. An accurate estimate is best obtained using a pH meter. An approximate estimate can be made in the field as outlined by this exercise.

Aim

To determine soil pH.

Materials

BDH soil-testing kit: marked glass tubes; BDH Universal indicator; distilled water; barium sulphate.

Time

5 min per sample.

Method

(a) Place about 1–2 cm of soil to be tested in the lipless end of the glass tube (see Fig. 38).
(b) Add 1–2 cm of barium sulphate. This helps clear the liquid by causing clay to flocculate and precipitate.
(c) Add distilled water to a level between the marker lines.
(d) Add a few drops of universal indicator.
(e) Put the cork in the top and shake the tube well.
(f) Allow to settle and compare the colour of the liquid with the colour chart provided.

Questions

(1) Why is pH important?
(2) What factors might be influencing the pH of the soil you have studied?
(3) What effect might pH be having on the distribution of organisms in the soil?

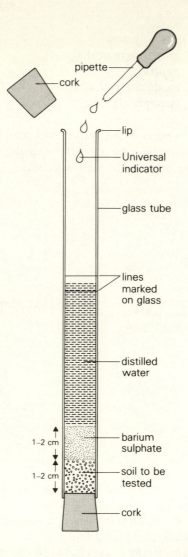

pipette

cork

lip

Universal
indicator

glass tube

lines
marked
on glass

distilled
water

1–2 cm   barium
sulphate

1–2 cm   soil to be
tested

cork

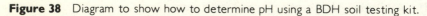

Figure 38   Diagram to show how to determine pH using a BDH soil testing kit.

Exercise 24: the water content of the soil

Background

Water in the soil is vitally important determining many of its properties
including structure, strength, expansion and contraction, as well as chemical
properties such as mineral weathering and the supply of available nutrients.
It also profoundly affects the biological state of the soil in terms of bacterial,
fungal and insect populations. Many of the organisms inhabiting the soil, for
example, protozoans, live in the water film around the soil particles.

Most of the plants of grasslands are **mesophytic**, which means that they are adapted to moist soil, as opposed to **xerophytic** plants that are found in dry conditions, or **hydrophytes** adapted to wet conditions. A lack of water may desiccate organisms, whereas waterlogging may cause anaerobic conditions to prevail. Flooding may help the dispersal of organisms. Many crops will not obtain their maximum yield unless an adequate supply of water is maintained.

The water content of the soil at any one time depends mainly on the following factors:

(a) climate: precipitation and evaporation rates are especially important. (See Exercise 20 on climatic factors).
(b) physical structure: this is determined by the way the small particles, e.g. sand, silt, clay, aggregate.
(c) texture: the relationship between soil texture and water content is as follows:

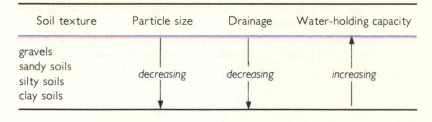

Soil texture	Particle size	Drainage	Water-holding capacity
gravels sandy soils silty soils clay soils	decreasing	decreasing	increasing

(d) topography: the gradient and the aspect of a slope are especially important. See Exercise 1.
(e) vegetation: this includes the nature and density of the plants present.
(f) water table: the level below which the soil is waterlogged.

The following is a simple method to estimate the water content of a soil. Soils should be collected as near to the same time as possible from different sites. The results from this exercise can be related to the populations of animals found in the soil (see Exercise 13).

Aim

To determine the water content of a soil.

Materials

Trowel; plastic bags; oven; heat-resistant mat; evaporating dishes; balance.

Time

2 h or more, depending on the type of soil. Sandy soils dry more rapidly than those with a high proportion of clay or organic matter.

Method

(a) Collect about half a trowel-full of soil from five different sites in the study area (see note at top of page 80).
(b) Place each sample immediately in a separate plastic bag to minimise water loss from the soil by evaporation.

Laboratory work
(a) Weigh a heat-resistant mat.
(b) Weigh five evaporating dishes.
(c) Weigh about 10 g of each sample into each evaporating dish.
(d) Place the dishes in the oven at 105°C and leave to dry.
(e) When the soil appears dry, weigh the dish and soil together, placing them on the heat-resistant mat on the balance.
(f) Return to the oven and reweigh after a further 20 min.
(g) Repeat step (f) until the weight recorded is constant.
(h) Calculate the percentage water content for each sample:

$$\frac{(N_1 - N_2)}{N_1} \times 100$$

where N_1 = initial mass of soil, and N_2 = final mass of soil.
(i) Calculate the mean percentage water content.

Questions

(1) How reliable are the results obtained? Discuss any factors that may be influencing them.
(2) If you have results for more than one site, what reasons can you suggest for any differences?
(3) What other important factor about the soil will be affecting the results?
(4) What influence might this have on the number and types of organisms present (see Exercises 13 and 16–18)?
(5) Devise an experiment to study the effect of different quantities of water in a grassland soil on the numbers and activities of organisms. See Exercise 13 for details of extracting animals from the soil.
(6) What use would a knowledge of the water content of a particular soil over a period of time be to an arable farmer?

Exercise 25: soil organic matter

Background

Organic material is the essential and characteristic part of the soil derived from plants or parts of plants such as dead leaves, roots and rhizomes, with small additions from animal waste products and dead bodies. It ranges from undecomposed plant and animal remains to an amorphous mass and provides an environment for denitrifying bacteria which help to return minerals to the soil in the process of decomposition. (See section on decomposition, p. 60). It also has a high water-absorbing capacity, lessening the problems of drought.

A problem that arises when measuring the organic content of a soil is the decomposition of inorganic materials, especially carbonates, when the soil is heated. One way to overcome this is to control the temperature to which the soil is heated. Soils of a high carbonate content, such as might arise in chalk or limestone grasslands, should be heated to a temperature of about 480°C, whereas low-carbonate soils can be heated to about 750°C. It is therefore useful to make a rapid assessment of the carbonate content of a soil as described below, prior to determining the organic content.

Aim

To determine the carbonate content of soil.

Materials

Boiling tube; 0.1 M hydrochloric acid; distilled water.

Time

5 min.

Method

(a) Put about 5 g of soil and a little distilled water in a boiling tube and shake to remove air bubbles.
(b) Add about 10 cm³ hydrochloric acid.
(c) Note effervescence (fizzing), if any. The following table will help you to make a subjective assessment of carbonate content.

Effervescence	Calcium carbonate content
moderate-strong	>5%
slight	1–5%
none	non-calcareous

Having determined the carbonate content of the soil, the following method describes how to measure organic content, by loss on ignition.

Aim

To measure organic matter in soil.

Materials

Crucibles; furnace; balance; heat-resistant mat; tongs.

Time

3 h for a soil with low carbonate content; 5 h for a soil with high carbonate content.

Method

(a) Using the dried soil from Exercise 24, weigh about 2 g of each sample into weighed crucibles, together with the heat-resistant mat, on the balance, and transfer to the furnace.

> N.B. Extreme caution is needed when handling the heated crucibles. It is better to sacrifice accuracy for safety.

(b) After 30 min, remove the samples from the furnace and weigh at once, placing crucibles on the balance on the heat-resistant mat.
(c) Return samples to oven for about 20 min.
(d) Repeat steps (b) and (c) until weight is constant.
(e) Calculate the percentage organic content in the same way as for water content (see Exercise 24).

Questions

(1) If you have results for more than one site, suggest reasons for any difference in quantities of organic matter.
(2) How could the number of earthworms influence the amount of organic matter present? Link this with Exercise 18.
(3) What effect will the temperature and climate have on the results?
(4) How meaningful are the results? What problems arise in trying to interpret them?

Exercise 26: soil particle size

Background

The size of the particles of a soil determines a whole range of other characteristics including drainage rate, aeration and temperature, and consequently the animal and plant populations present. All these factors will
affect the fertility of a soil and be of considerable importance to the arable
farmer. Sandy soils never support as many animals as those with high organic
matter or clay (see the introduction to this section). There are several ways
in which particle size of a soil can be determined, including the following
methods:

Finger assessment   A quick subjective assessment can be carried out in the
field by feeling the soil between the fingers and thumb (see Key 4).

Settling soil in water   Shake some soil in a straight-sided vessel, such as a
measuring cylinder, containing water, and the different fractions will settle
out.

Sieving   Dried soil is passed through a series of sieves, as described in this
exercise:

mesh size 72 mm diameter	>sand
mesh size 0.05 mm diameter	sand
mesh size 0.0018 mm diameter	silt
base (receiver)	clay

Aim

To determine the particle sizes of a soil by mechanical analysis.

Materials

Container for soil, e.g. plastic bag; trowel; evaporating dishes; mortar and
pestle; set of sieves.

Time

Several hours to dry soil; 30 min to sieve and weigh soil.

Method

(a)   Collect about half a trowel-full of soil from the area studied, or if
carrying out Exercise 24, use the remainder of this soil.

(b)   Put the soil in evaporating dishes and place in the oven at 105°C.
(c)   When soil is completely dry, place about 500 g in a mortar and pestle and break up the soil into particles ready for sieving.
(d)   Assemble the sieves in order of decreasing mesh size, the coarsest at the top.
(e)   Place the soil in the top sieve and shake the sieves vigorously but with care, from side to side.
(f)   Weigh the soil on each sieve and record as a percentage of the total weight of soil sieved.

Questions

(1)   Describe the texture of the soil studied as deduced from the results obtained for particle size; Table 5 may be useful here.
(2)   Comment upon the method and any possible sources of error.
(3)   What kind of relationships might there be between particle size and animal populations in the soil? Link to Exercise 13 to test this relationship.
(4)   Relate your results to the aeration of the soil.
(5)   What effect will the particle size have on the water content of the soil? Devise an experiment to investigate this relationship.
(6)   Discuss the importance of soil particle size in relation to soil fertility.

Key 3: Scheme for finger assessment of soil texture
(From Burnham, C. P. 1980, *The soils of England and Wales. Field Studies* **5** (2), 349–63.)

1   Does the moist soil form a coherent ball?
      Easily.   **2**
      With great care.   **loamy sand** (but check using tests **2** and **3**)
      No.   **sand**
2   What happens when the ball is pressed between thumb and forefinger?
      Flattens coherently.   **3**
      Tends to break up.   **sandy loam** (but check using tests **3** and **4**)
3   On slight further moistening can the ball be rolled into a thick cylinder (about 5 mm thick)?
      Yes.   **4**
      No, collapses.   **loamy sand**
4   On slight further moistening can the ball be rolled into a thin thread (about 2 mm thick)?
      Yes.   **5**
      No.   **sandy loam**

5 Can the thread be bent into a horseshoe without cracking, e.g. around the side of the hand?

Yes. **7**

No. **6**

6 On remoulding with further moisture what is the general 'feel' of the soil?

Smooth and pasty. **silt loam**

Rough and abrasive. **sandy silt loam**

7 Can a ring of about 25 mm diameter be formed by joining the two ends of the thread without cracking? (If necessary remould with more moisture and begin again.)

Yes. **9**

No. **8**

8 On remoulding with further moisture what is the general 'feel' of the soil?

Very gritty. **sandy clay loam**

Moderately rough. **clay loam**

Doughy. **silty clay loam**

9 On remoulding without rewetting can the surface be polished with the thumb?

Yes, a high polish like wax with few noticeable particles. **10**

Yes, but gritty particles are very noticeable. **sandy clay**

No. **8**

10 On wetting thoroughly, how strongly does the soil stick one's fingers together?

Very strongly. **clay**

Moderately strongly. **silty clay**

Table 5 To show the proportions of particles in relation to soil texture.

Soil texture	Proportions (%)		
	Sand	Silt	Clay
sandy	>80		
silty		>50	<40
loamy	<80	<50	>40
clayey			>40
particle size range – diameter (mm)	2.0–0.05	0.05–0.002	<0.002

Bibliography

General ecology

Bennet, D. P. and D. A. Humphries 1974. *Introduction to field biology*. London: Edward Arnold. (Excellent information both about ecology and how to study it in the field. Some useful background reading on grasslands.)

Cloudsley-Thompson, J. L. 1974. *Microecology*. London: Edward Arnold. (An introduction and practical guide.)

Krebs, C. J. 1978. *Ecology, the experimental analysis of distribution and abundance*. London: Harper & Row. (Very useful reference book for ecology in general.)

Lewis, T. and L. R. Taylor 1967. *Introduction to experimental ecology*. London: Academic Press. (Includes quantitative ecological exercises, information on the analysis of data and techniques. Useful insect key also.)

Odum, E. P. 1975. *Ecology*. London: Holt, Reinhart & Winston. (Very useful general ecology reference work.)

Sankey, J. 1958. *A guide to field biology*. London: Longman. (A practical approach. Includes methods, and a section on project work.)

Southwood, T. R. E. 1966. *Ecological methods*. London: Methuen. (Very comprehensive book on quantitative sampling. Largely related to the study of insect populations.)

Plant or grassland ecology

Ashby, M. 1961. *Introduction to plant ecology*. London: Macmillan. (Good background reading; covers biotic and abiotic environment and the nature of plant communities.)

Crothers, J. H. and A. M. Lucas 1982. Putting the biology students out to grass: the Nettlecombe experiment after thirteen years. *J. Biol Educ.* **16**, 108–14. (Useful background to Exercise 6.)

Etherington, J. R. 1978. *Plant physiological ecology*. London: Edward Arnold. (This covers the interpretation of plant behaviour and distribution in terms of physiological responses to the environment. Useful general reading.)

Kershaw, K. A. 1974. *Quantitative plant ecology*. London: Edward Arnold. (Useful reference text.)

Moore, I. 1966. *Grass and grasslands*. London: Collins. (Invaluable background reading.)

Spedding, C. R. W. 1971. *Grassland ecology*. Oxford: Oxford University Press. (Useful background text.)

Tivy, J. 1971. *Biogeography. A study of plants in the ecosphere*. Edinburgh: Oliver & Boyd. (Useful for Exercise 8 in relation to plant succession.)

Willis, A. J. 1973. *Introduction to Plant Ecology*. London: George Allen & Unwin. (A completely revised edition of Sir Arthur Tansley's book of the same name. Very useful text for vegetation, soil and climate work.)

Wilson, R. W. and D. F. Wright 1972. *A field approach to biology. Unit 1 the playing field*. London: Heinemann. (Contains much practical information.)

Animal ecology

Delany, M. J. 1974. *The ecology of small mammals*. London: Edward Arnold. (Includes some practical methods for mammal study.)

Dowdeswell, W. H. 1959. *Practical animal ecology*. London: Methuen. (Includes some practical techniques and their application in animal ecology.)

Gurnell, J. and J. R. Flowerdew 1982. *Live trapping small mammals. A practical guide*. Berkshire: the Mammal Society. (Essential for mammal trapping. Useful also for identification.)

Soil ecology

Burnham, C. P. 1980. The soils of England and Wales. *Field Stud.* **5**, 349–63. (Contains the 'Scheme for finger assessment of soil texture'; see Exercise 26.)

Jackson, R. M. and F. Raw 1966. *Life in the soil*. London: Edward Arnold. (Useful for soil ecology. Includes practical studies.)

Mc. E. Kevan, D. K. 1962. *Soil animals*. London: H. F. & G. Witherby. (General introduction to the study of soil fauna, including life histories, methods of sampling.)

Wilson, R. W. and D. F. Wright 1972. *A field approach to biology. Unit 4: soil studies and disturbed areas*. London: Heinemann.

Texts having useful sections on decomposition

Cloudsley-Thompson, J. L. 1974. *Microecology*. London: Edward Arnold.

Nuffield Foundation. 1966. *Teacher's guide 1 and Text 1: introducing living things*. Middlesex: Longman/Penguin.

Nuffield Foundation. 1966. *Teacher's guide and Text 4: living things in action*. Middlesex: Longman/Penguin.

Statistics

Bailey, N. T. J. 1980. *Statistical methods in biology*, 2nd edn. London: Hodder & Stoughton. (Readable book, covering a range of useful statistics.)

Identification guides

Burton, J. 1968. *The Oxford book of insects*. Oxford: Oxford University Press. (Illustrations and brief description of insects. Very useful for the section on 'animal analysis'.)

Chinery, M. 1972. *A field guide to the insects of Britain and northern Europe*. London: Collins. (Includes a key to insect orders. One of the most useful books available.)

Clapham, A. R., T. G. Tutin and E. F. Warburg 1981. *Excursion flora of the British Isles*. 3rd edn. Cambridge: Cambridge University Press. (Keys and descriptions of clubmosses, horsetails, ferns, conifers and flowering plants.)

Cloudsley-Thompson J. L. and Sankey J. 1961. *Land Invertebrates*. London: Methuen. (A guide to invertebrates other than insects commonly encountered in the field.)

Fitter, R., A. Fitter and M. Blamey 1978. *The wild flowers of Britain and northern Europe*, 3rd edn. London: Collins. (Useful, has illustrations and brief descriptions.)

Hubbard, C. E. 1984. *Grasses*. 3rd edn. Middlesex: Penguin. (The guide to grasses. Excellent illustrations and text.)

Keble Martin, W. 1982. *The new concise British flora*. London: Ebury Press and Michael Joseph. (Attractive illustrations, useful for identification. Arranged in families.)

Miles, P. M. and H. B. Miles 1968. *Chalkland and moorland ecology*. London: Hulton Educational Publications. (Useful practical suggestions, keys and illustrations.)

Moreton, B. D. 1950. *Guide to British insects*. London: Macmillan. (Illustrated account of the structures and life histories of insects. Descriptions of insect orders and keys included.)

Phillips, R. 1977. *Wild flowers of Britain*. London: Pan. (A series of coloured photographs of flowers throughout the year. Brief descriptions.)

Phillips, R. 1980. *Grasses, ferns, mosses and lichens of Great Britain and Ireland*. London: Pan. (Photographs of grasses could be particularly useful.)

Index

Note that common names are presented here in their 'natural' order, e.g. 'red fescue', *not* 'fescue, red'.